Please renew/return this item by the last date shown.

So that your telephone call is charged at local rate,
please call the numbers as set out below:

	From Area codes 01923 or 0208:	From the rest of Herts:
Renewals:	01923 471373	01438 737373
Enquiries:	01923 471333	01438 737333
Minicom:	01923 471599	01438 737599

L32b

LADY DENMAN, G.B.E.

1884-1954

By the same Author

★

Talking of Tea

Endymion Porter
The Life of a Courtier
1587–1649

Trudie Denman, *circa* 1935

Lady Denman, G.B.E.
1884–1954

Gervas Huxley

1961
CHATTO & WINDUS
LONDON

Published by
Chatto & Windus Ltd
42 William IV Street
London WC2

★

Clarke, Irwin & Co Ltd
Toronto

Printed in Great Britain by
Ebenezer Baylis & Son, Ltd., The Trinity Press
Worcester, and London

AUTHOR'S NOTE

For many years I was privileged to enjoy Lady Denman's friendship. If this has made the task of writing her life a labour of love, it has also added to my responsibility. In its discharge, however, I have been immensely helped by Lady Denman's daughter, Lady Burrell, who asked me to undertake the work and who gave me access to all her mother's papers as well as to the rich store of her own memories. I am also greatly indebted to the Hon. Clive and Mrs Pearson and to Mrs Margaret Pyke for reading my manuscript, for the loan of letters and for many valuable suggestions. Many other relations and friends of Lady Denman have been kind enough to help with recollections and letters given to me or to Miss Barbara Bliss, the fruits of whose careful and patient research, culled both from documents and from interviews, have provided so much of my source material and have so greatly aided my task. She and I would particularly wish to thank the Hon. Mrs John Hare, the Hon. Mrs Grant, Lady Barlow, Lady Wavell, Freda Lady Listowel, Lady Albemarle, Lady Dorothy Mennell, Miss Nancy Tennant, Lady Henley, Lady Sanderson, Dame Frances Farrer, Mrs Inez Jenkins, Miss Joy Winn, Mrs McCrindle, Mrs Diggle (formerly Lady Barttelot), Dr Wilberforce and Mr W. R. Derwent. Special thanks for help are also due to Mr H. L. White of the Commonwealth National Library at Canberra, to the Hon. Ronald Mack, member of the Upper House of the State Parliament of Victoria, to the Secretaries of the Bush Nursing Centres of the State of Victoria and of the New South Wales Bush Nursing Association, to the Librarian at the Office of the High Commissioner for Australia in London, to the Secretary of the Carnegie United Kingdom Trust and to the Warden of Denman College.

CONTENTS

PLATES

CHAPTER I

Origins

So short is memory that we even take for granted changes that have come about in our own lifetime. Today no one questions that women have an equal right with men to education, to intellectual freedom and to opportunity to serve the community. We forget that only seventy-five years ago, when the subject of this biography was born, the vast majority of Englishmen still firmly believed in the mental, moral and physical inferiority of women, and were convinced that child bearing and ministering to men were the two essential objects of a woman's being. Even in the home and family circle which bounded a woman's influence, women had only just ceased to be legally regarded as nonentities, dependent on their husbands' charity. The idea of marriage as a partnership of equals was almost completely strange. Female education was based on such concepts. Women were not admitted to degrees at Oxford and Cambridge, and, as T. H. Huxley wrote,

> 'girls have been educated either to be drudges or toys, beneath man; or a sort of angels above him . . . that women are meant neither to be men's guides nor their playthings, but their comrades, their fellows and their equals, so far as Nature puts no bar on that equality, does not seem to have entered into the minds of those who have had the conduct of the education of girls.'

Domestic service, the lowest paid and usually sweated labour in a few classes of industry, nursing and, for the best educated, elementary teaching or the post of a governess or companion were the main occupations open to single women. The professions were an exclusively male preserve; there were no women in business, even as typists and secretaries, far less as executives; none in the Civil Service. Women had not acquired the local

Government vote, and were unrepresented on County or other Councils and local bodies. The Parliamentary vote for women and membership of Parliament were still over thirty years ahead.

Many forces both material and spiritual helped, in an era of change, to bring about this so-recent revolution in the status and outlook of women; many leaders helped to organize and consolidate the victory. In one important sphere, at least, no one person was to contribute more than Gertrude Denman, born Gertrude Mary Pearson in November 1884, the second child and only daughter of Weetman and Annie Pearson, who were later to become the first Viscount and Viscountess Cowdray.

Both her father and her mother were of Yorkshire stock. On her father's side, her great-grandfather, Samuel Pearson, had left the farm in 1844 to become a working partner in a small Huddersfield building and contracting firm. Twelve years later, with his eldest son George, he founded the contracting firm of S. Pearson and Son. The firm prospered and George moved to Bradford. He married a Yorkshire woman, Sarah Weetman Dickinson, and their eldest son, Weetman Pearson, Gertrude's father, was born in 1856.

Weetman grew up strong in health, and self-reliant and industrious in character. At school in Harrogate he showed a bent for mathematics and mechanics. In 1872, when he was 16, he entered the family business. At the age of 23 he became his father's sole partner on his grandfather's retirement, working with his men on many drainage projects. When, in 1884, the firm moved its headquarters to London, Weetman Pearson, aged 28, became, in effect, the head of the business. His success was immediate. Within five years he had placed S. Pearson and Son in the front rank of contractors, and before the end of the century Weetman Pearson had completed or was carrying out contracts to the value of over £25,000,000, a figure which would represent some £150,000,000 in terms of today's money values. At home these contracts included great engineering works for docks and harbours and for railways, as well as the Blackwall tunnel under the Thames. Overseas, harbours and docks, canals and railways were built in Canada, the West Indies, Egypt, Mexico and Spain.

Pearson had also undertaken the most difficult and dangerous part of the Hudson River Tunnel in New York, on which American contractors had failed. Later he was also to build for New York its East River Tunnel.

A fresh and major interest came to Weetman Pearson with the new century in the development of oilfields in Mexico. Great electrical enterprises were also undertaken in the shape of light and power supplies and tramways in Mexico and elsewhere in South America, while Dover harbour was one of his notable home contracts. During the First World War Pearson was made responsible for the construction and management of perhaps the largest single enterprise undertaken in Britain, the huge munitions factory at Gretna, complete with housing for 20,000 workers. After the war, the firm's most notable achievement was the building of the Sennar dam on the Nile, which laid the economic foundations for the Sudan by providing water for cotton growing on the Gezira plain. At home, in partnership with Dorman Long, Pearson created a new Kentish industry in the development of the East Kent coalfield. Newspapers also became an important post-war interest with the conversion of the Liberal evening newspaper, the *Westminster Gazette*, into a morning paper and its subsequent amalgamation with the *Daily News*. The largest interest in a group of provincial newspapers was also acquired.

Weetman Pearson was a staunch Liberal in politics. Free Trade, Home Rule for Ireland, Women's Suffrage, Old Age Pensions and Sickness Insurance were amongst the causes dear to him. He was elected Member of Parliament for Colchester in 1895 and held this marginal seat for fifteen years. But he found the life of a Member of Parliament, with its desultory, time-wasting hours at Westminster, ill suited to an active and orderly man of business and he resigned his seat in 1909. In 1894, at the early age of 38, he had been created a Baronet. In 1910, he was raised to the peerage as Baron Cowdray of Midhurst. Seven years later he was made a Viscount and a Privy Councillor when, for a short time, he joined Lloyd George's wartime Government as President of the Air Board.

Weetman Pearson died in 1927. His phenomenal success had

been wholly due to his own outstanding qualities—to his untiring labour, his mastery of detail combined with a genius for organization, his perseverance and inexhaustible patience, and his judgement, with courage and caution equally mixed. The advice that, in 1903, he gave to his nineteen-year-old daughter about her behaviour in the hunting field summed up the line that he himself took in business. Rumour must have reached him that she was riding too boldly. 'There is always the happy mean,' he therefore wrote, 'the true point between nervousness and timidity and courage and rashness. One extreme is as bad as the other. Hence you should avoid both.' Nine years later, in the midst of some of his most difficult and critical oil negotiations in Mexico, he ended a long letter to his daughter with a description of the philosophy which guided him.

'Dame Fortune,' he wrote, 'is very elusive; the only way to succeed with her is to sketch a fortune which you think you can realize and then go for it bald-headed. The headaches, the fears, the ceaseless work (which starts each morning as if nature had not been exhausted the night before, but existed in inexhaustible generosity), the endless disappointments that will be met not only each day but many times a day, the sacrifices (thousands of them) that have to be made, all become incidents that have to be overcome and forgotten. Then Dame Fortune, wooed in such a manner, usually succumbs.'

Weetman Pearson's goal was much more than the acquisition of great personal riches. His pleasure and his adventure lay in his work, in overcoming difficulties and dangers and in seeing grow, under his hand, great enterprises that increased the wealth of the world. His character was simple and straightforward; his outlook broad and generous. A good employer, he took a personal interest in those who worked for him, and labour difficulties were largely unknown in his firm. Characteristically, it was the subject of labour relations that he chose for his Rectorial address at Aberdeen in 1920. In his view, the crux of the matter lay in the share that labour should justly receive for its contribution to production. Neither communism, nor socialism and nationalization of in-

Trudie, aged 7

dustry seemed to him to give the answer. The solution that he put forward was piecework with a guaranteed minimum wage, a bonus on profits and a share in management, together with a national scheme of unemployment insurance.

As is often the case, there was a very close bond between Pearson and his only daughter, his 'Trudles', to whom he was devoted. Her admiration of him was immense, and, of all his children, she was perhaps the most like him in character and outlook.

In 1881, when he was 25, Weetman Pearson had married a Bradford girl, Annie Cass. John Cass, her father, was born in 1832 and, like the Pearsons, came of Yorkshire farming stock. The Cass family moved to Bradford in 1840, and at the age of 13 John Cass went to work in a stuff merchant's warehouse. Some twenty years later he started his own small cloth manufacturing business. Taking an active interest in local politics on the Conservative side, he was elected to the Bradford Town Council and became Chairman of the Bradford Conservative Association and a Justice of the Peace, being knighted in 1897 for his political services. It was thought locally that Weetman Pearson had made a good match.

Annie Pearson was a little woman of indomitable spirit and great force of character. In her devoted husband's eyes she was the perfect wife and partner. His 'needed life blood', he called her in a tribute he wrote shortly before his death, 'one who shares with head and heart the successes and the failures, who gives the encouragement but has the courage to administer the home truth unpalatable but necessary sometimes, who is never afraid of responsibility.' It was in the tradition of Yorkshire wives that she should help her husband as a partner in his enterprises. She often accompanied him abroad, sharing rough food and quarters and exposure to all weathers, and with her care guarding his health against the typhoid, malaria and yellow fever which in those days took such a toll of life in Central America. Like her husband she was a stalwart feminist, and brought her belief in partnership with men into the Women's Movement, becoming for many years an active member of the Executive of the Women's Liberal Federation. Her own talents for organization found expression in her work for the nursing profession, where she played a leading and most generous part in the establishment and building of the College of Nursing, and, with her husband, presenting the Cowdray Club for nurses in Cavendish Square. But Annie Pearson was also possessed of a driving social ambition, a determination, with her husband's wealth and achievements, to surmount Victorian and Edwardian barriers of caste, and, despite snubs and set-backs, to become a leading political and social hostess. To the successful fulfilment of this ambition she devoted much of her remarkable energy and talents. As a parent she drove and harried her children along the road of her ambitions. Her love for her daughter, which was great, made her the more critical when Trudie failed to live up to her own particular standards. These were indeed high, but were based on the values that alone seemed to her to be important.

Such were the origins of Gertrude Pearson. Her whole life was to be inspired by the example of her father, to whose character and principles she owed so much more than to the wealth with which he endowed her. If, on the one hand, she was also to owe much to the atmosphere of a home where the wife was no pale Victorian shadow of her husband but an active partner in his interests and pursuits with a full life of her own as well, it was, on the other hand, her strong reaction against the social and material standards which her mother tried so relentlessly to force on her that was to help build up her own very different values; her indifference to worldly success or social status or money; her love of the simple things of life; her dislike of pretensions and pomposity; and her interest in people just as people.

CHAPTER II

Childhood and Adolescence, 1884–1901

Weetman and Annie Pearson had just moved to London when their daughter was born in 1884. Harold, their eldest child, was two years old. The new baby was christened Gertrude Mary, to be known as 'Trudie' by her family and friends throughout her life. The Pearsons had bought 4 Durham Villas (now re-named 4 Phillimore Place), a modest little house in the pleasant but un-pretentious neighbourhood of Campden Hill; but in a year or two the family moved to a larger house on top of the hill, 16 Airlie Gardens, a tall grey-brick Victorian abode. Two more sons were born to complete the Pearson family, Clive in 1887 and Geoffrey in 1891.

The London of Trudie's childhood has changed beyond any-thing then imaginable. It was still the London of horse transport. The well-to-do had their own broughams, victorias and landaus; for public use there were the four-wheeled 'growlers', musty-smelling from the straw on their floors, and the dashing two wheeled hansoms, both summoned by the whistle kept on the table in the hall of every London home, one blast for a hansom and two for a four-wheeler. Along the Bayswater Road to the north of Airlie Gardens and along Kensington High Street to the south, trundled the rival buses of the Road Car Company and the London General Omnibus Company, each pulled by two sturdy horses. Children favoured the former since they flew a little Union Jack by the driver's seat, but in either case a child could scramble up the stairs to the open top and make for the front seat (all seats had heavy black mackintosh rugs for wet weather) to talk to the driver about his horses. The Metropolitan railway provided the only mechanical transport. Running partly below ground, its steam trains heralded their arrival at Notting Hill Gate or High Street Kensington stations by blinding clouds of black smoke issuing from the tunnel. Although there was far less traffic, London was a noisier place than it is today. The beat of the horses' hooves and the clanking of iron-rimmed wheels were so penetrating, even in residential areas, that straw had to be thickly littered outside houses in which there was serious illness in order to deaden the noise. This was a custom of special interest to children who would pester nurse with their speculations about the precise nature and gravity of the illness. Other vanished noises then familiar to children were the cries of the street hawkers, the tinkling notes of the barrel organs grinding out the latest popular tunes, and the melancholy strains of the 'German Bands', parties of three or four itinerant wind instrumentalists, attempting more classical airs.

In those days, in the social class reached by the Pearsons, the children's world was mainly that of the nursery and the servants' hall. Contact with parents was usually confined to the evening when, washed and changed, the children would be escorted by Nannie to the drawing-room to spend an hour with their mother until Nannie's knock at the door called them back to the nursery, supper, bath and bed. The Pearson children saw even less of their parents than did most of their contemporaries. Their father's business enterprises involved both him and their mother in long absences abroad, while the claims of the Colchester constituency, first unsuccessfully contested in 1892 and then won by assiduous nursing three years later, took up much of Weetman and Annie's time when they were in England. The nursery and servants' world was, however, a full one. Even in such an upper-middle-class home as Airlie Gardens, seven or more servants would be kept; nurse and nurserymaid, cook, butler or parlourmaid, housemaid, kitchen maid and between maid—at a total cost in wages of under £200 a year. For the Pearson children there was, too, Miss Dickinson, a governess who came by the day and kept Trudie and Clive busy with a scrapbook ('it was such fun,' Trudie wrote to her mother), or took them for walks in Kensington Gardens across Church Street with its crossing sweeper, a shabby old man with a broom who earned a humble living from the pennies of his clients by sweeping the mud off the road so that the ladies' trailing skirts should not get soiled. Then there were riding lessons in Rotten Row and, for Trudie, dancing classes to

Trudie, aged 13

Lady Pearson
with her silver bicycle

attend at the Academy kept by the formidable Miss Wordsworth. One of her eyes was reputed to be of glass, but with the other she was terrifyingly quick to single out and discipline clumsy or inattentive pupils in the Lancers, Valse, Polka or Highland Schottische. In the winter months there were many children's parties with dancing, conjurors and Punch and Judy shows. There were, too, other children's homes to visit for play and tea. A letter from Trudie, aged 7, to her mother described how she 'went to Mrs Cooper's and when I was at the door I could not ring the bell but I saw a little boy and he rang it for me. When I got in we skipped and rode on a rocking horse and then we played at horses. I enjoyed myself very much.' Perhaps it was because of the difficulty of reaching door bells that Trudie's Nannie—highly class conscious as all Nannies were—told her that 'little ladies don't sit down on doorsteps, but wait for the front door to be opened by the butler.'

Trudie's tenth year—1894—was memorable in the Pearson family for two events. Her father was made a Baronet; and he bought a country house and estate. It was Paddockhurst in Sussex, and consisted of a large modern stone house with 3,000 acres of woodland and farmland. Adjoining the house Sir Weetman built palatial stables, home farm, sawmill and fire station whose amateur firemen regularly won the county competition.

Paddockhurst provided Lady Pearson with all the necessary country house atmosphere and occupations for social and political entertaining, although the ladies of the county were at first doubtful as to whether they should call on her, and some took a long time before they did so. But the Pearsons were excellent hosts and the Paddockhurst parties were greatly enjoyed by the numerous and distinguished guests whose names soon began to fill the visitors' book. Furnished houses in the country for the summer holidays had hitherto given the Pearson children their only taste of country life. Now they had their own country home, with farms and woods, ponds and lakes, gardens and tennis lawns, and ponies of their own to ride. For Trudie, Paddockhurst was the first real introduction to the life of the countryside which was ever after to mean so much to her. At first it was bicycles that furnished one of the Pearsons' main country pursuits. The new 'safety' bicycle, with its two nearly equal wheels, had just been introduced, superseding the old 'penny farthing' and enabling women for the first time to ride bicycles. The comfort and speed of bicyling had also been revolutionized by the invention of the pneumatic tyre. So, in the nineties, a bicycling craze swept the world, and even smart London society took to practising riding bicycles in Hyde Park. At Paddockhurst all the Pearson family learned to ride bicycles. Lady Pearson's bicycle was made of solid silver. Sir Weetman and Lady Pearson had seen this unique specimen in the window of Tiffany, the famous jeweller, when they reached the luxury of New York after months of hardship and discomfort in Mexico. He had presented it to her as a nice tribute to her care of him.

The advent of the era of the bicycle was commemorated by a frieze designed by Walter Crane which ran round the Paddock-hurst dining-room. The frieze depicted the development of transport through the ages, from early man with his skin boats, pack horses, waggons, the coach, the railway, to finally, as the culminating point, the bicycle, with Sir Weetman and Lady Pearson standing beside their mounts. At the end, the frieze also showed, in very small size, a few embryonic motor-cars, but the artist was clearly doubtful as to whether such a means of transport was likely to be of any future importance.

Back in London Trudie was sent to a day school in Queen's Gate. Her school report for the Easter term of 1897, when she was 12, shows her third in a class of nineteen. She had never once been late, had lost no marks for bad conduct and had gained high marks for neatness and attention. Her only bad report came from the German mistress. The report must have been more flattering than truthful, since, in later life, Trudie always said that she delighted in behaving badly. While she was still a pupil, the school moved from London to Ascot. Trudie was offered the chance of going with it as a boarder, but refused. She said later that she much regretted this cowardly decision.

It may well have been in order to help correct the weakness in her German that in August 1897 Trudie and her elder brother

Harold were sent in charge of a German Fräulein on a bicycling tour down the Rhine. Trudie kept a diary which meticulously recorded each day's travels, sights and adventures. Although she was the youngest of the party, it was Trudie who woke up the others for the early starts; and it was she who bound up Harold's knee when he had a nasty fall on a muddy road. She showed, too, prudent care about money. They chose to stay at a cheap inn by the roadside to avoid the expensive hotel at Bonn; they were disappointed when they found no fourth class on the railway and had to travel third; they claimed a refund of two shillings when they missed the fast train and had to take a slow one. The weather was often wet and they spent much time cleaning and oiling their 'bikes'. In the evenings they played whist. Trudie's diary is that of an observant person. The descriptions of the roads, scenery and castles are clear and vivid, but to her practical mind the most interesting sights were the women and not the men working in the fields, and in the castle at Heidelberg, 'the noted barrel holding 49,000 gallons of beer; it has been filled three times, the last time was in the 16th century.'

The next year, 1898, brought another important change in Trudie's background, when the Pearsons moved from the modest neighbourhood of Campden Hill to aristocratic Carlton House Terrace. Here, at number 16, Lady Pearson had full scope for London entertaining on the grand scale. Her attack on Society had politics for its base. The Liberal Party was out of power. The Home Rule issue had alienated many of the great Whig families and had led to the Liberal Unionist split. 'They count as Tories,' observed Lady Bracknell of the Liberal Unionists in Wilde's *Importance of Being Earnest*, first staged in 1895. 'They dine with us. Or come in the evening at any rate.' But if Tories and Liberal Unionists were unlikely to grace Lady Pearson's parties, Annie succeeded in making 16 Carlton House Terrace an important centre for Liberal social gatherings at a time when such entertainment played a leading role in political life. Her invitations embraced both the 'Little Englanders', led by Sir William Harcourt, and the 'Liberal Imperialists', the followers of Lord Rosebery, who included Asquith, Sir Edward Grey, Lord Cromer and

Haldane. It was to this latter group that Weetman Pearson adhered, but within the Liberal party he was known as a peace-maker, devoid of ambition for office for himself, whose judge-ment was much valued in the Party's inner circle. Liberals of both factions met accordingly at Carlton House Terrace and at Paddockhurst.

Carlton House Terrace provided, however, a somewhat bleak existence for a girl in her early teens, whose parents were often abroad for long periods. Even when they were at home, her father was, of necessity, absorbed in his ever expanding business in-terests, while her mother was engrossed in her social-cum-political activities. Harold and Clive were both away at boarding schools and Geoffrey was only seven years old, so, except in the holidays, Trudie was very much alone with the governesses who were now entrusted with her education. 'It was clever of Lady Pearson to get Lady Crewe's governess for Trudie, to teach her the ways of the world' recalled one of her mother's contem-poraries. But Trudie disliked all her governesses, especially a German one who kept a monkey and made Trudie look after it. She was frightened of the dark and the big house held terror for her when she was sent up to bed alone. Like many lonely children she became an omnivorous reader, not only devouring the Classic English novels, but also tackling books on economics, philosophy and history. Herbert Spencer was her guide in philosophy, while, in history, Prescott's Conquests of Mexico and Peru held a special appeal owing to her father's Central and South American interests. Outside books, she found companionship among the servants, notably with Mrs Bell, the cook, a woman of fierce temper but sterling honesty of character, and at Paddock-hurst with Argent, the coachman, with whom she spent much time in the stables. She had a dog so devoted to her that to everyone's embarrassment he would even sit waiting for her outside the lavatory. But her dog died, and Trudie, heartbroken, vowed that since dogs did not live as long as humans she would never have another. It was a resolve that she kept all her life.

In January 1901, a sixteen-year-old Trudie was taken by her parents on a trip to Mexico, staying in New York *en route*. Later that year she was sent to a finishing school in Dresden. She preserved the letter that her father sent to her there on her seventeenth birthday.

'My dear Girlie,' it ran, 'I must write tonight so that you get my heartfelt good wishes for a many happy returns of the day at the proper time—for breakfast on your birthday. May you, my dear Trudie, enjoy all blessings for a many many years, a treasure to us always as now. Seventeen is an important year, probably one of the most, when you begin to feel mature and take a greater interest in womanly than girlish things. 'Tis the turning point and Mother and I can only pray that the future may be as satisfactory as the past. We can desire nothing greater. . . . My business—I know you are interested in it—goes on as usual. Daily troubles and daily successes. Immediately after Christmas I should leave for Mexico.'

In Dresden Trudie attended life-classes at an Art school and frequented the opera. A week before she came home for Christmas she wrote to her mother,

'I hope that I shall be able to hunt the Wednesday after I arrive and not stay in London too long? . . . I have a splendid idea for skating at Paddockhurst; if it acts we shall get some nearly every day.' 'I hope you are enjoying your parties,' she added as a postscript.

It is easy to see where Trudie's tastes lay. Up till then, a tomboy at heart, she had enjoyed boys' recreations with her brothers, but Lady Pearson felt that the time had now come to divert some of her energy and ambition into the work of launching her seventeen-year-old daughter into Edwardian Society.

CHAPTER III

Coming Out and Marriage

It was a formidable ordeal for a girl of seventeen to be launched into the fashionable world under the aegis of so ambitious and critical a parent as Lady Pearson. Trudie dutifully accepted her lot, although she afterwards recalled with misery the long, tight clothes she had to wear, and the boredom of the lengthy and elaborate meals. Apart from her own Carlton House Terrace and Paddockhurst parties, Annie carefully organized her daughter's London social life and her visits to other country houses. The trunk that the lady's-maid packed with the many clothes needed for the week-end (women were expected to change their dresses before lunch, before tea and before dinner) also carried round a large album. This the débutante had to fill with the signatures of fellow guests, and adorn with photographs or old prints of the house visited, enlivening the pages with verses, sketches or witty remarks contributed by her more talented friends. Trudie's album covering the summer and autumn of 1902 was meticulously kept.

A letter (though of a few years later) from a guest tells of a typical week-end party at Paddockhurst.

'There is a large party here, which shifts and changes, as some went on Saturday and were replaced by others. Mildred and Mr Buxton, the Freddy Guests, Mr Holland, a daughter of Lady Jersey and her husband, Lord Aberdare, an Irishman, Lord Doneraile, a violinist (name forgotten, he only came last night), Lady Cory, Lady Carew, Lord and Lady Edmund Talbot, several of the Pearson family. Also several people came in to dinner every night. . . . Lady Pearson is most friendly. As for Sir Weetman, I couldn't have imagined how interesting—thrilling—can be the accounts of tunnel building and the lives of the men employed on it and his description of the Mexican oil wells.'

For Trudie's benefit, some of the Paddockhurst parties were

devoted to entertaining her own contemporaries. In a letter which Sir Weetman sent from Mexico City to Trudie in January 1903, he referred to her description of the Christmas house party at Paddockhurst for young people which had been 'amusing, rowdy, enterprising in its pleasures and ambitious in the hunting field'. The party had gone round the neighbourhood singing carols—the neighbours had *not* been amused—and Trudie had complained that her efforts as a carol singer had only earned her twopence. 'That twopence,' wrote her father, 'ought to be treasured as now you will know what earning money means. There are many twopences that *every* successful man (or woman), whatever their careers may be, has to work as hard for as you did for yours.'

Sir Weetman's long letter shows how he sought from his own experience of men and affairs to advise and influence his daughter. ' 'Tis always well,' he wrote, 'to remember that a reputation is a most dangerous possession. Those who own it have, willingly or unwillingly, the almost irresistible temptation to live up to it. The beautiful woman takes to dyeing and generally touching up (by adding to or taking from—in the latter case so far, of course, as possible) in her thirties or forties; the brilliant woman must shine at whatever strain or effort to herself or perhaps misery to others at being made to appear ignorant or foolish; the rich must continue to spend when possibly they would be much happier (and truer to their own interests) by being careful; the bold rider has often to take foolish chances for fear of being considered commonplace; and so *ad infinitum*. No! The only true course to follow is to remain as near commonplace and average as your surroundings will allow you. This conduct will save many heartburnings, many disappointments and many false positions. But, at the same time, it is necessary to have large reserves, so that at any time you can push your way to the front should it be necessary or advisable to do so. This line of conduct brings respect and love and "gets you there at the finish". Hence be careful to avoid having nothing behind. If you can make a splendid show in the window, do so, so long as there will be no disappointment when the interior of the shop is examined.'

Trudie preserved this letter and was to follow much of its

advice. Certainly, the stock that she kept behind the counter was always far more than appeared in her shop window.

Her father's letter also contained a revealing passage about her mother. 'I do hope,' he wrote, 'that mother is feeling herself again. Her happiness controls very largely her health. If her nerves are unstrung from any cause, she gets below par at once. Make it your care to see that she keeps above par.' It was an injunction that was, very shortly, critically to influence Trudie's loving and dutiful heart.

Young men were beginning to play a part in Trudie's life and her father showed his interest in them. Of one, he wrote approvingly that 'he would never be found wanting'; of another, he knew that he could rely on his 'daughter's tastes running to something more mature and ambitious'. But already Trudie's future husband had entered the scene. In November 1902, a photograph of Lord Denman appeared for the first time in one of the groups at Paddockhurst in Trudie's album. Trudie's first sight of him had been when her mother took her to a ball in London. As she mounted the grand staircase she saw Denman standing on crutches at the top, a romantic figure of a wounded officer from South Africa. He was a young Liberal peer, the twenty-eight-year-old third Baron Denman. The first Baron had, as an advocate, distinguished himself in 1820 as one of the counsel for Queen Caroline's defence in her trial in the House of Lords on the charge of adultery. Becoming Attorney General in 1830, he was made Lord Chief Justice two years later, being raised to the peerage in 1834. Thomas Denman the third Baron, was the son of an unambitious and far from wealthy Sussex squire, and had inherited the title from his great uncle in 1894, when he was 20. His childhood had been passed in the unhappy atmosphere of a broken home, his mother, a hard and ambitious woman, having divorced his father, then divorced a second husband and then re-married for the third time. He had always been delicate and a martyr to asthma and hay fever. Nevertheless, he had gone through Sandhurst (in the same year as Sir Winston Churchill) and had entered the army, serving with gallantry in the South African war before being wounded and invalided home. He had then decided to go into politics, and, on the shrewd advice of his uncle, Bishop Wilberforce, had chosen the Liberal side. In July 1902 he had made a much-praised maiden speech in the House of Lords.

Thomas Denman had good looks and charm. He was courteous, with gentle manners, cultured and witty, an excellent horseman and fond of and proficient at all games. He was also able and ambitious. Lady Pearson saw in him a desirable match for her daughter; a man of suitable birth and breeding, who, backed by her influence and Pearson money, should go to the top in politics and help forward her dynastic aspirations. Denman, if also moved by material considerations, fancied himself passionately in love with the intelligent, gay and attractive girl of 18. Trudie's nose, whose aquiline shape had been made more pronounced by being broken in a rough game with her brother Harold at Paddockhurst, deprived her of any claim to classic loveliness, but throughout her life the look of kindness, humour and transparent honesty in her blue eyes gave her face a beauty which in her youth was enhanced by a wonderful complexion, set off by red-gold hair. There was, too, great charm in the quality of her low, clear voice. Her figure was slim and boyish, with broad shoulders and narrow hips, though such figures were not yet fashionable; and while she had a fine slender leg for a boot, her strong hands had not the feminine delicacy then admired. One of her great attractions must have been that she was such a good listener, genuinely interested in and sympathetic to any one who was not affected nor a *poseur*. Another must have been her infectious sense of humour, always appreciative of other people's jokes and always ready to make a joke herself.

Trudie was entirely inexperienced. Her mother's dominating and critical character had made her painfully shy and unsure of herself; and she was warmly affectionate and anxious to please those she was fond of and to whom she felt she owed a duty.

Denman's courtship went on through the spring and summer of 1903, aided and abetted by Lady Pearson, 'the old mother, such a worldly old cat,' as she described herself in a letter to

Denman. Trudie was attracted to him as an amusing friend and
companion. But when he proposed marriage she refused him,
writing:

'I never thought you were serious till the dance last Friday. I
thought we were very good friends and rather amused each
other and that was all. I am afraid I was very stupid not to
understand. I am sure you will meet lots of better people than
I, so please don't be downcast by what I fear is my hardness of
heart. I hope this does not stop my being always your friend,
Trudie Pearson.'

Denman and Lady Pearson were not, however, to be dis-
couraged, and the courtship was pressed on. Lady Pearson's health
became a factor influencing Trudie who remembered her father's
injunction. 'Mother is not getting braced as I had hoped and still
looks rather worried,' she wrote to Denman from Braemar
Castle in Aberdeenshire, which the Pearsons had leased for the
summer. 'It suddenly struck me last night that you and I might
be a bit responsible for it. I never thought of it before, but it
is extraordinary how Mother feels things.' Denman, too, in
despondent letters, preyed on her feelings.

Finally, in August, Denman came to stay at Braemar Castle.
There the engagement took place. If a deep and mutual falling in
love was not the mainspring of the match, neither was this the
case in many, if not most, of the successful society marriages
arranged in days when girls of 18, brought up like Trudie, were
accustomed to follow the accepted convention that 'Mother
knows best'. The strength and persistence of Denman's wooing
had certainly made Trudie believe that he was whole-heartedly in
love with her, and her own generous and affectionate nature
made her feel that she ought to be able to respond. Much later in
her life Trudie was to give this advice to her daughter. 'Never get
married unless you are certain that you would be *absolutely
miserable* if you said No. That is the best way a girl can test
whether she is really in love or only thinks she may be.'

The three months between the engagement and the wedding
were very busy ones for Trudie. There were sittings for photo-

graphs, a profusion of household goods to buy, and endless trying on of clothes, while, all the time, the wedding presents poured in to Carlton House Terrace, to be methodically listed as they arrived in the special little red leather book which Trudie kept for this purpose, and to be promptly acknowledged. There were over 300 of them. Trudie disliked all the fuss. 'I have spent a slightly more useless 24 hours than usual since you left,' she wrote to Denman. 'I don't mean that I have been slack, but trying on clothes and telling people how much I like presents that I really think awful does not strike me as a profitable occupation'.

The wedding took place on November 26th at fashionable Saint Margaret's, Westminster. On her wedding morning Trudie told her mother that she felt that she could not go through with the ceremony. But Lady Pearson firmly quelled this last-moment and quite impossible attempt to escape from the net. The service was conducted by the Bishop of Chichester, assisted by three other clergymen. There were five grown-up bridesmaids, in golden brown velvet with muffs of black fur, and three child attendants. The Press reporters lavished their superlatives on the magnificence of the occasion. They admired Trudie's 'masses of red-gold hair' and described her as 'unusually clever'. Never, they wrote, had such crowds of guests been seen at a wedding as at the reception at Carlton House Terrace, where a colossal bell of white flowers entirely filled the well of the staircase, while another flower bell, equally huge, hung in the drawing-room, and where the bridesmaids arrived from the church in an omnibus painted in the bright yellow of Sir Weetman's electioneering colours. So great was the throng, it was reported, that many of the guests could not get further than an inspection of the wedding presents, which were headed by the magnificent jewellery showered on the bride by her family. Her parents' gifts included a rope of 400 splendid pearls.

Trudie's wedding clothes were fully illustrated in the fashion papers. For the ceremony she wore a very tight-waisted gown of ivory white velvet and old Brussels lace, with a Juliet cap of seed-pearls in place of the usual orange-blossom. Her going-away hat, which was surmounted by a stuffed brown owl with glass eyes, was particularly admired.

The wedding had 'a soupçon of New York about it', observed one newspaper. It was also noted that the bridegroom had a bad cold and looked very ill.

A shooting party at Paddockhurst, 1903
Queenie Quirk (later Countess Wavell) with scarf in centre;
Trudie in corduroy suit on right

CHAPTER IV

Women's Suffrage

A hunting box in Warwickshire had been lent to the Denmans for their honeymoon. On their return they occupied a flat in 16 Carlton House Terrace, placed at their disposal by Sir Weetman and Annie. They also rented a country house in good hunting country near Leamington. Thomas, their eldest child, was born at Paddockhurst in 1905. Mother and new-born baby had measles. Both were so critically ill that Harold Pearson drove in record time to the nearest hospital to fetch oxygen. That year Sir Weetman bought his daughter her own country estate. It was Balcombe, in Sussex, a 3,000 acre property, marching with Paddockhurst. The house, Balcombe Place, which was to be Trudie's country home for the rest of her life, had been built in the 1850's in stone in an innocuous Victorian-Tudor style. Inside the rooms were large and pleasant. The estate included two other houses, eighteenth-century Balcombe House, and Stonehall dating from Charles II. There was a home farm (which was let until after 1918), other farms, much woodland and about a hundred cottages, including part of Balcombe village. So great, at that time, was Trudie's passion for hunting that her first reaction to her father's gift of an estate in an undistinguished hunting country such as Sussex was one of grief. Later she realized how wise he had been not to indulge this excessive absorption, and, instead, to choose a spot where the land was beautiful and unspoiled and yet accessible to London. It was not long before she was deeply attached to the house and the land. Farming was never to be of real interest to Trudie, but she loved the woods and took a very keen personal interest in the well-being of her tenants. At once, she began to busy herself with improving her cottages and giving them water and sanitation—rare cottage luxuries in those days. Her second child, Judith, was born at Balcombe in 1907. Trudie was too young and immature fully to appreciate her babies, and her pregnancies were unhappy times of feeling ill, looking awkward and being deprived of the pleasures of riding and playing games.

Denman took an active part in the House of Lords, sometimes acting as Chief Liberal Whip. He hoped to be given an Undersecretaryship, but it was a court appointment that came his way in 1905, when he was made a Lord in Waiting to the King. Two years later he was appointed Captain of the Corps of Gentlemen at Arms. Denman's activities involved a good deal of entertaining, both at Balcombe and in London. In 1909, the Denmans left their flat at 16 Carlton House Terrace and set up their London establishment at 4 Buckingham Gate, a house conveniently close to the Palace with big public rooms for entertaining. At Balcombe in the winter there were large pheasant-shooting parties which Trudie had to help organize, and the house was often filled with week-end guests. The visitors' book for 1906 to 1911 includes the names of such Liberal leaders as Campbell-Bannerman, Winston Churchill, McKenna, Augustine Birrell, Simon and Lords Crewe and Willingdon. J. A. Spender was also a regular visitor.

No one more enjoyed the company of friends than did Trudie, but she had no social ambitions. Although she took much trouble over helping her husband's career through her entertaining, her own inclinations were to escape from social duties as far as possible. Dancing and large parties were things to be avoided, and calling on Sussex neighbours alarmed and bored her. She used to go round returning cards driving a disreputable old governess cart, pulled by newly-broken Welsh ponies. Her companion was often Nellie Grant, a young married woman whom she met in 1907 and who soon became one of her closest friends. Stonehall, only a few hundred yards from Balcombe Place, was leased to the Grants. Once, when calling on some very dull and proper neighbours, Trudie and Nellie had come to the end of their conversational resources after the current Royal Academy picture exhibition had been exhaustively discussed. Seeing Trudie scratching her head in agonized search for a fresh topic, Nellie innocently asked, 'Oh, Lady Denman, do you etch?'!

But even if Sussex was not the Shires, there were hunts to be enjoyed with the Crawley and Horsham and Southdown packs. Trudie was a good horse-woman riding side-saddle, but she preferred quiet, well-schooled hunters, particularly in the cramped country of that part of Sussex which she found so much more alarming to ride over than the open Warwickshire fields. Recalling those days, Mrs Grant tells of one memorable occasion when she and Trudie went out with the Warnham staghounds, and the Master and his wife arrived at the meet in a four-wheeler, both roaring tight. Most of the field also got drunk at a large hunt breakfast, and when the stag was let out, everyone rode as hard as they could in different directions. Since the only safe place seemed to be in front, Trudie and Nellie, riding all out, led the field for twenty minutes, after which the huntsman called off the hounds and fed them with biscuits while the stag was returned to its box. Trudie and Nellie then hurried home to play in a hockey match. Hockey in winter and lawn tennis in summer, at both of which Trudie was very keen, were the main amusements apart from hunting. Sawing trees and lopping branches and making bonfires was also a pursuit which Trudie greatly enjoyed to the end of her life. There was, too, her motor car; and Trudie became one of the very early lady drivers. To her early married years also belongs a caravan tour one July in Somerset and Devon with two friends, one a young married woman and the other a girl in her teens, Alicia Knatchbull-Hugessen, who was later to become her sister-in-law. They picked up the caravan, the 'Westward Ho', with its driver and two horses at Taunton and proceeded by leisurely stages into Devonshire and to the sea; camping at night near farms and all greatly enjoying the novelty of doing their own camp cooking, although all three found the washing up a chore. Caravanning was then almost exclusively confined to gypsies, and the farmers looked on the three young women as harmless lunatics, but an old lady threatened to report them to the R.S.P.C.A. when she saw them whacking the lazy horses with cold frying pans in a despairing effort to make them pull. Trudie carried a pistol which gave the party a great feeling of security. The only time it was handled was one middle of the night when the caravanners woke to hear loud breathing and rattling outside. Gingerly picking up her pistol, Trudie opened the door, to find that the cause of the disturbance was only an old cart-horse snuffling at the latch. But Alicia woke to another alarm when one night Trudie, in the upper bunk, dozed off when reading Beatrice and Sydney Webb on local government; and the heavy tome crashed to the floor, narrowly missing Alicia asleep in the lower bunk. It is nostalgic to note from the diary kept by one of the party that the farmer's charge for Devonshire cream, milk, butter and eggs for the three of them and for fodder for the horses and use of the land for their camp for the night amounted in all to 7s. 6d.

From the start, Denman's wretched health overshadowed Trudie's married life. In the summer his hay fever compelled him to seek relief in sea voyages; in the winter his bronchitis forced him to spend weeks in bed and at Cannes. During the first summer of their marriage, Trudie went with her husband on a yachting cruise, but she was a bad sailor and did not enjoy it. The next summer Denman voyaged to the Cape and back. In loving letters to her absent husband, Trudie described herself as 'miserably lonely' and referred to their 'dreadfully long separations'. She had already acquired the habit of heavy cigarette smoking—in those days it was considered daring for a woman to smoke at all—and her letters told how she had reduced her cigarettes to three a day for fear of the bad effect of more on her pregnancy.

Soon after her daughter was born, Trudie became involved in her first public work, when, in May 1908, she was elected through the influence of her mother to the Executive of the Women's Liberal Federation. The Executive had as its President and Chairman that awe-inspiring matriarch, Lady Carlisle; dictatorial, radical and imbued with such a fanatical zeal for Temperance that she was popularly, if erroneously, believed to have poured the complete contents of the Castle Howard cellars down the drains. Lady Pearson had been on the Executive for many years and other and equally formidable elder members were Lady Aberconway and Mrs Broadley Reid. Lady Carlisle, as head of the Federation, not only led an organization of close on 100,000

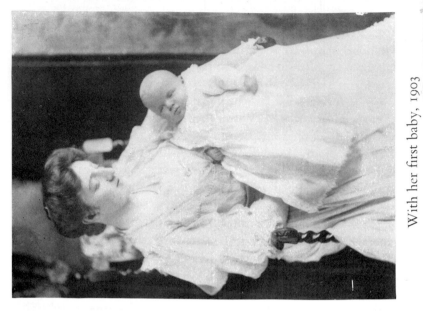

With her first baby, 1903

Presented at Court on marriage, 1903

stalwart, if still voteless, Liberal women in the Constituencies; she also had her own team of three Liberal members of Parliament from her family circle, a son, a son-in-law and her secretary; while on the Executive she had the support of two of her daughters. Under her leadership, the Women's Liberal Federation formed an important political body and pressure group.

The main question to which the Executive was now devoting its energies was that of Women's Suffrage. It was a question on which the women of Britain were themselves divided. The Women's Political and Social Union—the militant suffragettes—under the redoubtable Mrs Pankhurst were waging their campaign of violence for equal votes for women on the existing property franchise. Their policy was to attack any Government irrespective of party that failed immediately to enfranchise women. Since a Liberal Government was in power, they were bitterly attacking the Liberals. The Women's Liberal Federation was strongly opposed to the militants. Its policy was to follow constitutional methods and, as a Liberal organization, it supported the extension of the franchise in order that the inclusion of women might give the vote to the working man's wife and the mill girl as well as to the property-owning woman. But there were still many women who were opposed to any kind of parliamentary franchise for women, and, in 1909, a Woman's Anti-Suffrage League was formed with Mrs Humphry Ward, the novelist, and Miss Violet Markham as its leaders. Like the Women's Liberal Federation, these Anti-Suffrage women deplored the tactics of their militant sisters, but they also felt that the country was not ripe for any extension of the franchise and that women should take fuller advantage of the opportunities recently opened to them in local government before demanding the parliamentary vote.

When Trudie joined the Women's Liberal Federation Executive, Asquith, the new Prime Minister, had just promised a deputation of Liberal Members of Parliament that an Electoral Reform Bill would be introduced to extend the male franchise and that the Government would not oppose an amendment to give the vote to women, provided that the demand for women's suffrage had behind it 'the overwhelming support of the women of the country, no less than the men.' In the circumstances, Asquith's proviso obviously gave the Government an easy let-out, but the Executive of the Women's Liberal Federation professed themselves greatly encouraged and started making plans for a great Albert Hall meeting at the end of the year with Lloyd George as chief speaker.

All that summer of 1908, the Albert Hall meeting was the Executive's chief pre-occupation. The militants had now taken to assaulting Cabinet Ministers with pepper and dog whips. Much concern was therefore felt about Lloyd George's safety at the meeting, and Trudie seconded a resolution for the appointment of an ex-policeman as head steward with police pensioners to assist him. The very youthful, inexperienced and diffident Trudie was naturally content to play a minor role on a Committee of much older women dominated by such termagants as her mother and Lady Carlisle. While quietly absorbing much useful knowledge, she made no attempt to make a mark of her own, and did no more than second other members' resolutions.

The Albert Hall meeting duly took place in December 1908. Trudie sat on the platform with the rest of the Executive and nine members of the Government. The militants created such a disturbance that, for a whole hour, Lloyd George was prevented from speaking. But his personality gradually dominated the meeting and he was able, in the end, to deliver his whole speech, handling the interrupters with great skill, humour and patience.

Meantime, the Liberal Parliamentary party had formed a Woman's Suffrage Committee, which produced a Bill abolishing the property vote and giving full adult suffrage to men and women alike. Lady Carlisle's son, Geoffrey Howard, was to introduce the Bill in the Commons in March 1909 and when, beforehand he met the Women's Liberal Federation Executive, Trudie seconded a resolution supporting him, which was carried in spite of the opposition of two members who disliked the idea of adult suffrage. But Howard's Bill got no further than the second reading, Asquith intervening to say that a measure of this kind should be sponsored by the Government and should 'be carefully moulded under the stress of prolonged and deliberate parliamentary discussion.'

With the militants becoming ever more violent, public opinion was turning increasingly against the whole Women's Suffrage movement. Even though the Women's Liberal Federation passed resolutions condemning violence and militancy, many Liberal candidates refused to answer the Executive's test questions on suffrage. But Lloyd George's 'People's Budget', introduced in April 1909, brought a fresh issue to the fore and closed the Liberal ranks for the inevitable General Election. The better to support the Government, the Women's Liberal Federation now formed Area federations, and Trudie was made Chairman of the Women's Liberal Metropolitan Union. It was a tribute to her youthful ability. In this capacity she busied herself with special conferences to strengthen the organization of London women election workers, and it was recorded that 'the result of the working of the new area scheme in London was proving highly satisfactory.'

On the eve of the General Election Asquith repeated his former declaration about Women's Suffrage, and 199 Liberal candidates promised support to the movement. With the General Election of January 1910 over and the Liberals returned to power with a narrow majority, the Executive of the Women's Liberal Federation turned again to the suffrage question, and Trudie was active in supporting the Executive's refusal to support Liberal parliamentary candidates who were evasive in answering the test questions. At the Federation's 1910 Annual Council meeting, she was elected to the Executive with a greatly increased vote, and spoke in favour of a resolution to curtail the power of the House of Lords to veto legislation.

In the House of Commons, an all-party Committee on Suffrage was now set up, known as the Conciliation Committee. A Bill was produced based on the property qualification, and it was supported by the militants, who declared a truce from violence and organized peaceful parasol parades in Hyde Park. In spite of the limited nature of the proposed franchise, the Women's Liberal Federation Executive also decided to support the Bill, and Trudie seconded resolutions to this effect. At a demonstration in the Caxton Hall she also moved a vote of thanks to the Government for giving time for the Bill's second reading.

In the Commons, however, the Bill, introduced in July 1910 by a Labour member, received rough treatment not only from Conservatives but also from Lloyd George and Winston Churchill, the latter pointing out that the property franchise would enable rich men to enfranchise their wives and daughters by giving them property. He also drew an amusing picture of prostitutes enjoying the vote by virtue of their premises, and then losing it if they made a respectable marriage. This Liberal opposition killed the Bill.

At the time of the further General Election in December 1910, the Women's Liberal Federation felt that the House of Lords issue was paramount and did not harry Liberal candidates to promise suffrage support, although the militants had now resumed their former tactics of violence. Trudie took part in this Election, going to Eye where she spoke at twenty-four meetings and helped to get her brother Harold returned with an increased majority. In May 1911, another Conciliation Bill was introduced by a Liberal member, but it came to nothing as general Liberal opinion was hardening against increasing the anomalies under the property franchise. It was only after the experience of women's work in the war that the overwhelming support of men and women alike was secured, and women gained the vote.

But, at the end of 1910, Trudie was looking ahead to work in a very different field. Her three years apprenticeship on the Women's Liberal Federation had not, however, been wasted. As a young and impressionable woman she had been an actor in the midst of important events. She had learned the machinery and business of a big organization. She had watched a great leader in the Countess of Carlisle in action, intervening here, sending a letter there, pulling strings and interviewing Cabinet Ministers when needed. She had observed other women's strengths and weaknesses and how best to handle difficult and strong minded people of divergent views. She had been forced to master her innate diffidence and self-distrust in the company of older women

Trudie, 1908

whose capacity she rated as so much higher than her own, and had made herself conquer her terror of speaking in public. Above all she had been recruited into the thick of the battle for equality for women in what was still a man's world.

The new field to which Trudie was now looking was Australia. In December (1910) Denman had been invited by the Government to become Governor-General of Australia in succession to the Earl of Dudley. It was a tribute to the opinion held of the young Liberal peer's personality and ability, since he was only 36, far younger than any of his predecessors. He had no hesitation in accepting the post. It was one, however, that needed the support of large private means, since the salary of £10,000 a year would not cover expenses even with the exercise of the greatest economy. It was thanks to Trudie's fortune that Denman was able to accept the offer, while her father's generosity made sure that no financial considerations should cramp his Governor-Generalship. The news had been cabled to Lord and Lady Cowdray (Sir Weetman Pearson had been made Baron Cowdray in 1910) who were in Mexico. On Christmas Day, Cowdray wrote to Denman expressing their great delight at the high roles that their son-in-law and daughter were now going to fill and at the great prospects for the future. 'You would, of course, have to do the thing as well as it could be done—within reason—' wrote Cowdray, 'and all shortage up to £50,000 we shall be delighted to find.' He went on to give Denman shrewd advice about the selection of his aides.

It was no easy assignment for either the Governor-General or for his wife, especially for a wife so young as twenty-six-year-old Trudie. Australia was then, as now, a land of vigorous, outspoken politicians and newspapers, and of a tough, democratic, highly individualistic people where 'every man thinks that he is twice as good as another'. Australians were intensely loyal to the Mother Country, yet ever on the look-out to resent any hint of patronage and inclined to class all Englishmen of the upper classes as pompous and effete snobs. Special difficulties confronted the Governor-General as the symbol of the Australian Commonwealth, which had only come into existence ten years before. Many Australians

still considered the Commonwealth a disastrous experiment, since
Federation bore with unequal incidence on the six Sovereign
States composing it, which differed so widely in their geography,
their history, their economic structure and their natural resources.
The shared honour and sacrifice of the beaches of Gallipoli had
not yet created a new sense of Australian unity, and no Pearl
Harbour had come to bind all Australians together in the bond of
common danger. In 1911, the States still fiercely cherished their
rights and resented the encroachment of the Commonwealth
authority. Each State had its own Governor, directly appointed
by and communicating directly with Downing Street, and, as
Lord Dudley wrote to Denman in warning, one of the State
Governors was 'a bitter and untiring partisan of the States Rights',
who aspired to lead the State Governors in a constant fight
against the Commonwealth Government. Lord Dudley also warned his successor that the Federal Ministers were 'very suspicious
and jealous of the smallest interference or influence in their affairs'.
The Governor-General was not—as he now is—the personal
representative of the Crown only. In 1911 the Sovereignty of the
British Parliament over the whole Empire was still largely un-
impaired. It was Downing Street that appointed the Governor-
General, who in addition to representing the Crown, was also the
representative of the Home Government, which amongst other
things was solely responsible for the framing and execution of the
Empire's foreign policy. It called for no small degree of tact to
fill this dual role *vis-à-vis* Ministers who already felt the urge for
complete autonomy to which the 1914 war was to give such
impetus, and on which the 1926 Imperial Conference and the
Statute of Westminster was to set the seal.

For Trudie, her husband's appointment meant that her life
would be encompassed by all the formality, ceremony and
trappings that she most disliked. 'Tell Mother,' she wrote to her
brother Clive who was with his parents in Mexico, 'that I intend
giving my whole mind to collecting my clothes and developing a
"presence" by means of breathing exercises.' Australia meant, too,
that she would be cut off from her home, her family and her
friends—and Lord Dudley had written to Denman that 'it is very

difficult for the wife of the Governor-General to make friends among the ladies here and she is apt often to feel very lonely and dull.' Trudie would feel such loneliness more than most people because of her devotion to the small circle of her family—her brothers and her sister-in-law Beryl—and a few intimate friends. She knew how homesick she would be; nor, to help sustain her in a strange and distant land, would Trudie be afforded the all-important love and companionship of a happy marriage.

The fact was that she and Denman were hopelessly unsuited to each other. His frequent bouts of ill-health and his unself-reliant nature demanded the constant sympathy and support of a wife whose own ambitions and interests would be wholly fulfilled in giving him the home background of which his unhappy child-hood had deprived him. Instead, he had married a vigorous young woman, independent and forthright of mind and character, and brought up in a family tradition of strong self-reliance and of intolerance of moral or physical weakness. But if he was dis-appointed in her, and if she felt that she failed him, his own un-sureness of himself and his admiration for her judgement and ability continued to make him turn to her for advice in matters both great and small. Nor did she ever allow her wealth to cause any difficulties. It was always 'our' money, not 'hers'. And if there was no longer any real happiness in the marriage, this was kept strictly locked up in private. No hint of any differences was given to the world and, in public, each loyally supported the other with courtesy and consideration.

CHAPTER V

Australia

The Denmans left London at the end of June, travelling overland to Marseilles where they picked up their ship for the voyage by Suez. Their last weeks in London had been very busy ones. It was the month of King George V's Coronation, and there had been the Coronation itself to attend on the 22nd, as well as the State Banquet two days before in Buckingham Palace. Then the Cowdrays had given an immense farewell party to Denman and Trudie at Carlton House Terrace, and there had been a number of lunches and dinners for Denman. Andrew Fisher, the Labour Prime Minister of Australia, with some members of his Cabinet had come to England for the Coronation and for the Imperial Conference of 1911. This had given the Denmans the opportunity to meet Fisher and his colleagues. They came to Victoria Station to see them off. In the Denman party were Miss Quirk (later Countess Wavell), an old friend and contemporary who had frequently stayed at Balcombe and who went to help Trudie, and Denman's Military Secretary Sir Walter Barttelot and his wife who were Sussex neighbours. The two Denman children and the two Barttelot children were sent round the Cape so as to avoid the heat of the Red Sea, and arrived later. A key domestic staff of eleven persons from Buckingham Gate and Carlton House Terrace had been sent in advance, headed by the most efficient Mrs Yaldren, Lady Cowdray's own housekeeper. The Denmans took with them their personal servants and two carriages and three motor-cars. The State carriage was a grand affair to be drawn by four postillion-ridden horses, with two footmen perched behind. The carriages and cars were painted in claret, the Denman family colour; and the postillions, chauffeurs and footmen wore claret-coloured livery with silver braid.

The new Governor-General—the fifth in the eleven years since Federation—arrived in Melbourne on July 31st. The Federal

Government, led by Andrew Fisher with W. H. Hughes as his chief lieutenant, was the Commonwealth's second Labour administration. Under Fisher and Hughes the Australian Labour party was nationalist with a strong imperial flavour, in that imperial patriotism formed an extension of Australian nationalism. It was this Labour Government that introduced compulsory military service for defence and created the Australian Navy, while Fisher was the first to describe the British Empire as 'a family of nations'. On the outbreak of war in 1914, he at once pledged Australia to uphold the common cause 'to the last man and the last shilling'. Fisher's Government was also determined to guard the Federal position against any encroachment by the several States. From the first, Denman and Fisher liked and trusted each other, and their relations were close and cordial.

Australian newspapers were notoriously critical and outspoken, and their more radical section was always on the lookout for opportunities to attack and ridicule what they conceived to be manifestations of English flummery such as those inherent in the pageantry attached to the Governor-General's office. Although such papers referred to Denman as the 'Gee Gee', to Trudie as 'Her Feathers' and to the aides-de-camps as the 'helps', Denman and his lady were given a favourable welcome from the Press. The arrival as Governor-General of a young and progressive Liberal peer was a novelty that appealed to Australians, and Denman was able to write of his 'hearty reception' to King George, whose own experiences during his visit to Australia as Duke of York in 1901 led him to take a special and sympathetic interest in Australian affairs.

Denman also wrote to his aunt soon after his arrival in Australia that he found his 'temporary grandeur rather oppressive; it is disconcerting to find ladies curtseying to me, and I'm always forgetting to sit down in the drawing-room, as they are not supposed to sit down while I'm standing.'

In letters to her brother Clive, Trudie described her own new life.

'I am so grand,' she wrote, 'that I am not allowed to go to any

43

but epoch making functions of a national character. I have to avoid doing anything merely civic or parochial, as that is the department of the State Governors' wives. I am also too grand to go into a shop. Can you wonder that most of the Governors' wives are bored to tears? I have been to two race meetings where I am taken round by the stewards and given tips by all those in the know—result I have backed 7 horses, one of which came second and the rest nowhere and I have lost £15 . . . The people I like best are the Labour people. They are very simple and nice. The only troubles we have had have been about who gets the entrée at levées and suchlike details, about which the officials are touchy to a degree. You would laugh to see us walk into dinner; first 2 ADC's in coats with blue facings and gilt buttons. Then D., covered in orders, with his lady, then me with the most important man. The footmen are too beautiful in claret and silver lace (lots of it) and knee breeches.' 'Wherever we go people have to meet us,' she wrote a few weeks later; 'we went to a football match and were met by the Committee. It is the same at hospitals and picture galleries. The Committees are bad enough, but their female relations who know nothing about the things are the limit. When the things are run by women it is nice to be shown round by women, but not otherwise . . . It is such a strain wherever one goes finding people to whom one must be polite. But we generally get a day's racing or hunting each week and odd games of tennis and, when wet, we play hockey in the ball-room. This last amusement must on no account be mentioned.' A week later she was writing, 'We have an awful fortnight before us. We give a dinner of 70, a ball of ten or twelve hundred and a garden party of two thousand, besides attending other people's functions.'

The role which Trudie was called upon to play was one to which she was least temperamentally suited. 'Being with people you like,' Trudie wrote to her brother Clive, 'is the most excellent relaxation. Don't lose your taste for people.' But being Her Excellency, 'playing hostess to the mostest', was quite another matter, placing her continually on show to thousands of curious and critical eyes, making her the target of every sycophant and bore and cutting her off, as Lord Dudley had warned, from forming any real friendships with Australian men and women. Those she met were on their best behaviour. No one was natural, and it was so hard to get to know them as people. Moreover, the descendants of the upper class immigrant families who regarded Government House as the centre of their world were wholly unrepresentative of Australia's vigorous democracy. Equally untypical were the wealthy graziers whose vast sheep stations the Governor-General and his wife sometimes visited. The only close friends Trudie made were Madame Melba, 'much more human than most people' she called her, and Mrs Sanderson, a keen and good games player who was the English wife of a Melbourne business man.

Trudie's job, too, was an exhausting one. Her official entertaining was on such a large and generous scale that, even with Lord Cowdray's financial help, she was alarmed at the expense. 'We spend money like water,' she wrote, and again, 'Everything is frightfully expensive (except mutton). It makes one (the expense not the mutton, I mean) a confirmed free trader.' Then there was the endless round of opening Shows and Exhibitions, the visits to schools and hospitals, the investitures and prize-givings and, on every occasion, the long-winded speeches so dear to Australians. The official visits to each State Capital were crammed with such functions. Arriving from Melbourne after long journeys by train or sea at the distant Adelaide or Brisbane, it seemed extraordinary to Trudie 'to find the same sort of people, speaking the same language and to drive through the same sort of streets with the same bungalows, crowned by the same tin roofs.' Describing their visit to Hobart, Trudie wrote, 'same old review of cadets, gave the same old garden party, went round the same old hospitals and met the same old people, at least they all seem the same people. The only new incident was that when we went to the Cathedral, the clergy met us at the door and we walked up the aisle with them, whilst the congregation stood; it was as embarrassing as getting married again. The chief surprise of the service was that the Dean preached a sermon about the Virgin Mary and the Governor-General. One flippant sailor says he fears that their names being coupled in this way will cause a scandal.' At Brisbane there were '6 functions a day on the average. Except in bed and when riding, I have been dressed up to the nines'—which to Trudie was especially hateful.

But Her Excellency showed no sign of any boredom in public, and, with her liking for and interest in people, she did her best to break down the barriers surrounding her. The almost uniformly favourable newspaper comment on her bearing shows how well she filled her difficult role. 'Lady Denman is a pleasant-looking lady' ran one typical comment, 'whom no one would accuse of beauty until she smiles. Her smile is a miracle, a whole wealth of kind-heartedness and good nature. . . . she went through the ordeal of introductions with the finest possible grace.' Or again, 'She does not adopt that pose of haughty disdain which has been so characteristic of some vice-regal ladies in the past. Besides, she smiles.' Although the newspapers considered her 'a famous dresser', the simple and comfortable clothes that she wore by choice set a new fashion among Australia's overdressed smart set. It was appreciated, too, that, as a newspaper wrote, she was 'unaffectedly friendly and sincere' and tried to make 'natural easy hospitality replace frigidity', and that her genuine desire to meet the people of Australia had introduced such innovations as Government House garden parties for 2,000 schoolchildren, and for 3,000 post office workers and their wives and children.

Trudie's experience on the Executive of the Women's Liberal Federation in their fight for the franchise gave her a special interest in women's organizations in Australia, where women for nine years had exercised the vote for both State[1] and Federal Parliaments. So beneficial had been the results that, early in 1911, the Australian Senate had passed a resolution setting out the good effect of the extension of the franchise to women and urging all nations enjoying representative Government to follow Australia's example. This had been cabled to Asquith. The most important woman's organization in Australia was the National Council of Women of each State. It was this Council's agitation that had secured the suffrage. Now its main concerns were over such

[1] Except in Victoria where women had not obtained the State vote until 1908.

Arrival at Government House, Melbourne, 1911

Front row, left to right: Lady Barttelot, Lord Denman, Trudie, Miss Queenie Quirk

matters as better pay and opportunities for women in education, the appointment of women magistrates, the medical inspection of schoolchildren, and better housing. Such issues appealed to Trudie's practical outlook; and one of her first public acts in Australia was to address the Victoria National Council of Women in Melbourne. 'This the first gathering of women I have met who are enfranchised,' she began her speech. Trudie met the National Council of Women in all the States, and the Victoria Council held their 1913 annual meeting in Melbourne Government House. At the first interstate conference of the Council, held in Sydney in July 1912, Trudie presided and stressed the value of the movement in moulding public opinion. Later that year she gave a foretaste of the interest which she was always to show in the constitution and structure of women's organizations when she suggested that the interstate conferences should be held every year so that the Councils in all the States could direct their work to the same objects.

At the farewell party which the National Council of Women gave to Trudie in May 1914, she made special reference to the kind of service that already appealed most strongly to her. In her speech, she asked the representatives of the fifty-two women's societies present 'to remember the wives of countrymen who worked to get the wealth of their families, but, unlike their men, had to work as hard at the end of life as at the beginning because of the lack of domestic help.' She spoke, too, of the toll on the health of countrywomen and their children. Of all her public activities in Australia, it was Bush Nursing that lay nearest her heart. This was a service to countrywomen and their families living in remote and scattered areas far removed from doctors and hospitals and skilled nursing, who had to struggle as best they could with illness and childbirth. Death was only too often the result. It was Trudie's predecessor, Lady Dudley, who in 1909 had conceived the idea of a self-supporting scheme in each State, by which Bush Nursing Centres would be established by local committees who would guarantee the cost of a trained nurse for their area. The scheme had encountered opposition from the medical profession in the fear that such nurses might take the place of doctors, but Madame Melba, fired by enthusiasm for the idea, had given a benefit concert which had raised £10,000 as the nucleus of a permanent endowment fund, half for Victoria and half for New South Wales.

When the Denmans arrived in Australia, only the first nurse had been appointed. This was in the remote township of Beech Forest in Victoria, and, because of the township's name, a beech leaf had been chosen as the Bush Nurses' badge. By the end of 1911 four nurses had begun their work, and one of Trudie's earliest activities was to attend a meeting of the Council of the Victorian Bush Nursing Association, when she undertook personally to visit some of these Nursing Centres and see their work for herself. Early in 1912 she fulfilled this promise, opening two new centres and installing the nurses by presenting them with their beech leaf badges. In a letter Trudie described one such installation.

'I had a four hours journey, a lunch there, speeches, a meeting, photographs, "God Save" by schoolchildren, and 4 hours back. As a matter of fact I rather enjoyed the day. They are so frightfully pleased to see one in the out of the way places, quite different from Melbourne.'

Next year (1913) Trudie presided at the Bush Nursing Association's annual meeting. There were now nine centres in Victoria, and Trudie lent her name to an appeal for further endowment funds because, as she wrote, 'the Bush Nursing Association was the only institution in Melbourne which worked for country-women.' Later that year on a riding and camping tour through the back blocks of Gippsland, she was able to see for herself the hardships and difficulties of the women in the lonely mountain and forest areas, and the devoted services of the Bush Nurses. They were on duty day and night and when on a case had to do everything for the sufferers. One nurse spent three months in a tent with her patient. Horseback was often the only means of transport. There were no ambulances, and operations had to be performed in the rough homes. The nurses also visited the schools, examining the children and giving lectures on First Aid and hygiene.

Recalling Lady Denman's visit in November 1913 to the new Bush Nursing Centre in Dargo, an octogenarian tells of his shock at seeing Her Excellency arriving dressed in riding breeches and smoking a cigarette. Never before had the remote little township seen a woman thus attired or smoking. The Mayor was so overcome that he had to keep his eyes averted from the spectacle as he delivered his address of welcome. The next day, Lady Denman and her party of three rode off into the mountains, Lady Denman refusing to take a tent saying that she had been longing to spend the night in the Australian bush, where cut branches of eucalyptus made a lovely spongy mattress. Unfortunately, a terrific thunderstorm broke that evening, but the two weather-wise local police who accompanied the party had taken their camping gear and the visitors were able to shelter in their tent.

Aided by Trudie's active interest and support, nearly twenty Bush Nursing Centres had been established in Victoria by the time the Denmans left Australia. Shortly after the First World War there were forty-seven Centres, while local hospitals and ambulances were being added to the service.

There were also two cultural activities in which Trudie especially interested herself in Australia. One was the Melbourne Repertory Theatre Club. Struggling with inadequate resources and playing in small halls, it put on plays by Ibsen, Shaw, Granville Barker, Galsworthy and Chekov. Trudie gave her full support to the Club, entertaining the company at Government House, attending their productions and aiding their efforts to raise funds. She also stimulated, if she did not originate, a project for the building of a Memorial Theatre to commemorate the tercentenary of Shakespeare's death. The theatre would have been the first National Theatre in the British Empire. It was to provide a home for the Melbourne Repertory players and was promised financial help by the Victorian State Government, but the project was killed by the war.

The other cultural activity which Trudie inspired was an Exhibition of old furniture, silver and china held in Government House, Melbourne in April 1914. Trudie took a keen interest in Australian crafts, particularly in woodworking and carving from the lovely native Australian timbers, but she was struck by the generally poor level of design. She therefore wanted the Exhibition to be of practical use to students at Australian colleges and to artisans.

As Chairman of the small exhibition committee, Trudie threw herself into the work of procuring the loan of exhibits. Over 500 were brought together, including many pieces of really fine quality. Madame Melba lent furniture from her collection, while the Denmans showed embroidery, tapestries, pictures and silver. Trudie herself wrote the historical foreword to the catalogue, based on Maquoid's History of English Furniture, and helped to arrange and label the exhibits. The Exhibition proved a great success. All expenses were cleared on the first day, and, in its life of ten days, it was visited by over 20,000 people, a profit of £1,100 being made for the benefit of the Melbourne Repertory Theatre Club and the Arts and Crafts Society.

Besides her own special activities, Trudie had, of course, to play her part as the Governor-General's wife in the important events of her husband's term of office. In one of these—the laying in March 1913 of the first foundation stone for the new capital of the Commonwealth—hers was more than a supporting role.

The Commonwealth of Australia Act of 1900 had provided that a Commonwealth seat of government should be established in territory belonging to the Commonwealth, and the States had agreed that this territory should be in New South Wales, but not less than a hundred miles distant from Sydney. It was not, however, until 1908, after long wrangling, that the Yass-Canberra district was chosen. The next year, the actual site for the new capital city was determined, and at the beginning of 1911 the Commonwealth assumed control of some 900 square miles of territory. That year the Commonwealth Government organized an international competition for the design of the new capital, but the Royal Institute of British Architects advised its members throughout the Empire not to compete, objection being taken to the conditions laid down, especially to the clause that the final award was to be in the hands of a layman, Mr King O'Malley, the Minister for Home Affairs in the Federal Labour Government.

He was a picturesque and forceful character of Irish and Scottish descent who had been born in Canada and brought up in the U.S.A. Because of the British boycott the competition became 'a competition of foreigners judged by mediocrities'.[1] One hundred and thirty-seven entries were nevertheless submitted from various parts of the world. The first prize was awarded to a Chicago landscape architect, Walter Burley Griffin.

Griffin's ideas were romantic and grandiose. They paid little attention to the functional aspects of a city and to such matters as the costs of roads and services. His aim was to make the fullest use of the mountains, to be seen as vistas at the end of long avenues with widely scattered groups of buildings reflected in ornamental lakes. As a report made by Sir William Holford in 1958 stated, it was 'as if the Civic Centre was on Kingsway, the Market Centre at Marble Arch, and the capitol on Primrose Hill'. 'Seven scattered suburbs in search of a city', is an Australian description of Canberra.[2]

King O'Malley was insistent that a start should be made on the new capital during the Labour Government's term of office, and that a formal opening ceremony should be held, even though the participants would have to camp out in the bush. The ceremony was to consist of the laying of foundation stones for a Commencement Column, an obelisk of granite from Great Britain, which was to stand on the slopes of Capitol Hill. This hill was the focal point of Griffin's whole design. On its summit a Capitol was to be built 'for popular reception and ceremonial or for housing archives and commemorating Australian achievement'. Denman fell in with O'Malley's plans and agreed to make the most of the occasion by himself performing the ceremony on behalf of the King with all the pageantry possible.

On March 11th (1913) the Vice-Regal party arrived at their camp, which consisted of small sleeping tents and a large marquee that had seen service in India at the King's Durbar. They were met by O'Malley who had spent the last weeks in the bush, helping to get the preparations made and often wielding pick and shovel

[1] *Australia*. W. H. Hancock.
[2] *Canberra, a Nation's Capital*. Edited by H. C. White.

himself. As he remarked, 'I had the dust, mud and slush, before it was time for the brass buttons and plush.' After a rehearsal of the next day's ceremony Trudie went rabbit shooting.

For some time the choice of a name for the new capital had been a matter of acute controversy. All sorts of names had been put forward, amongst them 'Sydmeladlperbrisho', which ingeniously if not euphoniously incorporated all the State capitals in one word. Denman himself favoured 'Southern Cross' or 'Myola' —a native word meaning a meeting place—but this latter suggestion had to be dropped when it was realized that its letters, transposed, could be made phonetically to resemble O'Malley. In the Federal Parliament O'Malley himself urged the adoption of 'Shakespeare' or 'Captain Cook'. Other suggestions were 'Pacifica', 'Fisherville', 'Denman', 'Radiance' and 'Austral'. The Cabinet eventually agreed on 'Canberra' after the existing name of the locality, but in view of the controversy they decided to keep their choice secret, even from the Governor-General, until the actual naming ceremony which Lady Denman was to perform.

March 12th dawned in glorious weather. There were 500 official guests, and nearly 5,000 people came in special trains from Melbourne and Sydney to the nearest station, whence they drove in cars, dog-carts, and waggonettes, or rode on horseback along a dusty road and tracks to the site. All brought hampers of food. With fireplaces and water-butts provided under the trees, a gigantic picnic was soon in full swing.

For the ceremony, the Third Light Horse Brigade, 1,000 strong, formed three sides of a hollow square. There were also two mounted bands, a battery of Field Artillery and a Guard of Honour composed of members of the Staff Corps and cadets of the Royal Military College. First, Trudie arrived, driving from the camp in a carriage. She was met by Fisher, the Prime Minister, O'Malley, Hughes and a number of Senators and was escorted to the Vice-Regal enclosure on the grandstand. Then the Governor-General in full dress cantered in on a charger, accompanied by two aides-de-camp and an escort of New South Wales Lancers. As soon as he reached the broken square the guns fired a royal salute and the bands struck up the National Anthem. After

Camping in the Bush,
Australia, 1912

Trudie
with Thomas and Judith,
Australia, 1912

Denman had laid the first foundation stone by tapping it with a gold and ivory trowel, the Prime Minister and O'Malley laid the second and third stones.

The moment had now come for the naming of the new capital. The name chosen was still a secret. Moreover, inside the Cabinet there had been considerable discussion as to how the name should be pronounced, some holding that the accent should be on the middle syllable, and others that it should be treated as having only two syllables. In their dilemma the Cabinet had decided that whatever pronunciation Lady Denman gave when she read out the name should be officially adopted. The chosen name was therefore written on a card which was placed inside a gold case. This was really a cigarette case engraved with the Arms of the Commonwealth. The donors knew of Trudie's addiction to cigarettes, but the Governor-General's wife was not supposed to smoke—certainly not in public. It was therefore officially a card case that contained the name.

Just at noon Mrs O'Malley stepped forward and presented the 'card' case to Trudie. The Prime Minister then invited her to name the new capital. Amid a fanfare of trumpets and with the bands playing 'All people that on earth do dwell', she walked to a dais. The music ceased. In a hushed silence she opened the case, took out and read the card, paused to look at the crowd and smile, and then, in her clear carrying voice, said, 'I name the capital of Australia Canberra.' She pronounced it 'Can-berra', putting the accent on the first syllable. There were loud cheers, and while the artillery fired a salute of twenty-one guns, the bands played 'Advance Australia' and 'God Save the King'. O'Malley then read out the cable which the Governor-General was to send to the King, 'I desire to convey greetings from the people of Australia to Your Majesty and announce that I have today laid the foundation stone of the Federal Capital City. Lady Denman has named it Canberra.' As Denman remarked in his speech at the official luncheon which followed, no one present was likely again to see the christening of the capital of a continent.

The commencement column for which the foundations were thus laid in 1913 has never been erected. The outbreak of the

1914 war put a temporary stop to development, and although in 1920 the Prince of Wales laid a foundation stone for the Capitol building, it was already clear that Griffin's ideas were too grandiose to be practical. His engagement was terminated, although his basic plan has broadly been followed. The Capitol has, however, never been built, and Capitol Hill failed to become the city's focal point. In 1936 the foundation stones for the column lay hidden under rank grass, a home for snakes and rabbits, but the site has now been cleared and made accessible, while a stone capping has been placed on the top of the three foundation stones, with a notice board giving a brief outline of the history of their laying.

Another important event during the Denmans' time in Australia was the start, in September 1912, of the construction of the Trans-Australian railway spanning the 1,000 miles of desert between Kalgoorlie in Western Australia and Port Augustus in South Australia. The Governor-General turned the first sod in a ceremony at Port Augustus. There was, too, the opening of the Commonwealth Bank, when Trudie's six-year-old daughter Judith performed the ceremony of printing the number on the first Commonwealth currency ten shilling note. Then there was the first Australian Antarctic expedition led by Dr Mawson, which owed much to the Denmans' influence and backing. Australia's Navy was also born during the Denman régime when, in 1913, the Governor-General and his wife welcomed the first ships of the Royal Australian Navy as they sailed into Sydney Harbour, and the Australian Naval Station was handed over by the Imperial Authorities. Denman was a strong supporter of the Australian naval effort. He was also greatly impressed by the Australian system of compulsory military training, established in 1909, which he went out of his way to encourage and to explain to the Home Government.

There was, however, one unfortunate and highly controversial event which added considerably to the Denmans' difficulties. This was their eviction from Government House at Sydney. The house had been built with British Government funds and had been completed in 1845. Since Federation, it had become the custom for the Governor-General to reside in Government House, Melbourne when Parliament was sitting, and to use Government House, Sydney for the rest of the year. It was here that the Denmans took up their abode in the autumn of 1911 and, at intervals, during 1912. But before the Denmans left London, the Labour Government of the State of New South Wales, at the instigation of the Attorney-General and acting Premier, Mr Holman, had announced their intention of turning Sydney Government House into a Museum and Public Park. The Commonwealth Government, also Labour, had, however, told Denman that the matter could be amicably settled by negotiation and had encouraged him to make the offer of arranging for the grounds to be open to the public at all times and the House itself and private gardens when the Governor-General was not in residence. Unfortunately Denman found himself caught in the toils of a bitter dispute inside the Labour Party. State jealousy of the Commonwealth was the main issue, exacerbated by personal rancour and rivalry between Holman and Hughes, who had been instrumental in getting commercial and industrial affairs placed under Federal control. Sides were taken by the newspapers and the public. Some Labour papers commented sarcastically that 'only the Fitzboodles would miss free cigars and wine on the tax payer' and called opponents of eviction 'toadies' and 'Messrs Yellowplush'. More sober press opinion tended to be indignant at Holman's behaviour, and crowded protest meetings were held under the auspices of the Lord Mayor. But Holman and his followers were adamant. In October 1912 the Denmans had to leave Government House for good. Denman issued a restrained and dignified message 'to the people', and he and Trudie were seen off at the railway station *en route* for Melbourne by an enthusiastic crowd of sympathizers, although, as Trudie wrote to her brother, the Denman party had thought that they might justifiably 'learn a real good curse out of the Bible' which they would deliver in chorus from their carriage windows as the train pulled out!

After the Denmans had left, a Citizens' Protest Committee was formed, while an angry crowd mobbed the New South Wales Ministers when they officially took over Government House in

December. The Citizens' Committee then took the matter to law and finally won their case in an appeal to the Privy Council, the decision being that Sydney Government House was Imperial property to which the New South Wales Government had no title. In 1915, therefore, the Union Jack was re-hoisted on Government House and the State Governor went into residence there.

The Denmans' life in Australia was not, of course, wholly occupied by the arduous round of state entertaining and state occasions, numerous as these were and conscientiously as they were performed. The Denmans also earned much popularity by the enthusiasm with which they entered into every kind of sport and game. Denman formed a most successful polo team, hunted, and jumped his own horses at shows. Trudie went out occasionally with the Melbourne Fox Hounds. There were alarmingly high log fences to be jumped and 'you have to gallop like mad over rough scrub full of rabbit holes', she wrote to her brother. 'At first I looked out for holes and saw hundreds everywhere, so after that I studiously refrained from looking near the ground and left it to my horse who dodged about and never put a foot wrong, and I enjoyed myself very much.' 'You had better not mention hunting to Mother,' she added in a postscript. Trudie learned, with some difficulty, to ride astride and took part in practice games of polo. Describing her efforts to her brother Clive, 'I don't often hit the ball,' she wrote, 'but I ride off with great success. They all laugh so when they see me coming that they often miss the ball, and I feel I am a real help to my side!' Tennis, which Denman played very well, was a stand-by. Trudie herself—also a competent player—took part in the Melbourne tournament, but after getting through three rounds in the mixed doubles, 'a large crowd and four cameras turned on me the whole time finished me off and I went absolutely to pieces.' But her sportsmanship was much to the taste of the newspaper reporters. So, too, was the novelty of a woman—let alone the wife of the Governor-General —driving her own motor-car 'with the cool nerve and superb presence that many sporting men would like to possess', as a newspaper commented.

It was in Australia that Trudie took up golf. 'I think that by starting now I shall be some good by the time I am 45,' she wrote to Clive. She soon became very keen. All the Government House party were given handicaps, and they and the children helped to dig bunkers for an improvised course in the grounds of Melbourne Government House. Tournaments were organized, one of which Trudie won by one stroke, 'but I am still the worst player in Australia,' she wrote, 'which makes me dreadfully sad.' At Sydney she started practising putting on the carpet in the drawing-room of Government House. This led to a competition round the house with cushions as bunkers. 'We broke one globe and one glass door, and gave a State picture a very nasty jar,' she told Clive, 'but we had the most pleasant evening since we have been here.' There were, too, visits to the seaside with the children and sailing and sea-fishing. Sorrento, sixty miles from Melbourne, was their usual resort. There they had a bungalow on the cliffs with steps leading down to a small pier and a bathing place enclosed by railings to keep out sharks. 'I spend most of the time being a good mother, sailing boats and digging in the sands,' wrote Trudie to her brother. There was fishing at night and Trudie described how she got her first shark, 'only a 5-foot one, but it was great fun; it fairly ran out with the line. I pulled it in and then shot it in the water with my revolver before getting it in the boat.' There was one holiday in North Queensland on a vast sheep and cattle station where the Denmans hunted kangaroo, shot emus and turkeys, drove cattle and learned to crack a stock whip. 'We have forbidden the owners to have a party,' wrote Trudie to her brother, 'or to give us anything to eat but roast chicken and rice puddings.'

What Trudie most enjoyed were the riding and camping tours. Denman disliked picnics, but she loved them and was never happier than when lopping branches and building bonfires.

'The brightest four days in Australia, as far as I am concerned, have just come to an end,' wrote Trudie after one such expedition. 'They were spent riding over mountains, sleeping at night in rest houses, where we cooked and washed up and did all the other things I really loved. The party, although vice-regal, didn't look it. I was neatly dressed in breeches, boots and flannel shirt; no collar, tie, skirt or any other impedimenta . . . I think we enjoyed ourselves even more than we should otherwise have done, because the holiday was immediately after Cup week which is absolutely the limit. In ten days we gave one ball (1,500 guests), one large dinner of 70 and one enormous garden party; and we attended two other balls, one other garden party and went four days to the races, driving in state. . . . each day we have luncheon parties and tea parties at the races which means still more talk.'

Trudie made, too, the most of the occasions when Denman and his staff were attending functions for men only. She and the other wives would then have a cosy evening in her boudoir with an informal meal of macaroni cheese, occupying themselves by entering up the press-cutting book. After a state occasion Trudie and the wives would have a competition to see how many names of the guests they could remember with an appropriate description for each. But Denman's health was no better. He was constantly in bed with colds and asthma, and Australia proved even worse than England for hay fever. Australia's national flower, the wattle, was a special cause of trouble. Loaded with yellow pollen it set off the Governor-General's hay fever like a spark to gunpowder, and, so far as possible, it had to be banned from being used as a decoration at his public appearances. All this illness made him moody and difficult so that the atmosphere of Government House was strained and charged with the fear of giving offence; and offence was just what Trudie was always inadvertently giving with what her sister-in-law once called her 'elemental simplicity', that was incapable of understanding such pettiness as taking umbrage at what anyone said. Denman's appetite for sympathy was insatiable and although Trudie never failed him in practical kindness and nursing care, it all imposed a heavy extra strain on her. Nor were matters made easier by the contrast presented by one of Denman's staff, a man of great charm of character who shared all Trudie's tastes and who made her feel that there was someone worthwhile who really admired her and was interested in her as a person in her own right. Lacking the intimate companionship of a happy marriage, she grew more homesick than ever for her family and friends in England. She disliked, too, the general atmosphere of casualness and slackness which seemed to her to pervade Australian life, especially when Australians were wont to compare themselves to hustling Americans and to denigrate England as slow and decadent.

Even Trudie's robust health began to falter under the combined burden of public duties and private strain. By May 1913, she was so tired and had lost so much weight that it was decided that she must go back to England for rest and recuperation. When she returned to Australia via Canada in September, her brother Harold and his wife Beryl altered all their own plans in order to accompany her back and to give her in Australia the comfort and support of her own family. Alicia Knatchbull-Hugessen, ten years younger than Trudie, who had been one of her companions on the caravan holiday, also went with them. The journey across Canada was much enjoyed, especially a stay at Banff, with swimming in the hot sulphur baths, and riding in the bracing mountain air of the Rockies. Trudie had recovered a stone in weight, and the new arrivals made the Government House atmosphere much easier for her, although her return at once signalled a spate of fresh entertaining and being entertained. She wrote cheerfully to her brother that

'D. and the kids are very pleased to see me again, which is all to the good. Thomas is a nice lad and can at last read, and at arithmetic he is rather a pro. Judith is a very cheerful child. Altogether I am very fond of them just now.'

In August, while she was in London, Trudie had seen Harcourt, the Colonial Secretary, and had hinted to him that her husband was anxious to resign. Harcourt at once wrote to Denman hoping that he would change his mind. 'You are doing so admirably well in Australia,' he said, 'that I should find it most difficult and indeed almost impossible to replace you.' The Prime Minister sent a message to the same effect. But Denman had made up his mind, and early in November he cabled Harcourt asking him to accept his resignation, saying that 'he was desirous of returning home next [July 1914] on completion of three years service as Governor-General.' In his cabled reply Harcourt accepted the resignation as from the date suggested. No Governor-General had, in fact, ever lasted out his full five-year term and only one had stayed more than three years. It was only natural that Denman should desire not to be absent any longer from affairs at home, and his health was also an important factor in his decision. Nor had the Governor-General's official position been made easier as the result of the Federal General Election in May 1913, when Fisher, the Labour Prime Minister, with whom Denman had always been on such close terms, found himself in a minority of one in the House of Representatives, although Labour had a majority in the Senate. Denman had summoned Joseph Cook, the Liberal leader, to form a government, but after Cook had appointed a Speaker, he was left without a majority and the ensuing stalemate prevented any business being done and left control in the hands of the Labour majority in the Senate. It was clear that a constitutional crisis was ahead, but by remaining at his post till next July Denman hoped to be able to see it through.

At the end of November, however, Harcourt cabled again to say that he had found a successor who would relieve Denman in May. To this Denman answered that it was advisable on public grounds that he should remain until the completion of his three years in July. He wished to avoid his successor being faced on arrival with the responsibility of using the royal prerogative to grant a double dissolution (of the Senate and the House of Representatives) as the only way out of the constitutional crisis. In fact, this was precisely what Denman's successor, Sir Ronald Monro Ferguson, was compelled to do in June. But Harcourt's only response was a cable repeating that it was necessary for the new Governor-General to arrive in Australia about the middle of May, and Denman's request for some explanation was met by a further cable that the middle of May was the latest possible date.

The most likely reason for this cavalier treatment by the Home Government would seem to lie in Denman's support of the Australian viewpoint on naval policy.

In 1909, the Admiralty had urged that, for the protection of

Naming Canberra, 1913

Left to right: King O'Malley, Trudie, Andrew Fisher, Lord Denman
and Arnold Quilter

Imperial interests in the Pacific, Australia should make herself responsible for a complete fleet unit, with capital ships as well as lighter vessels. Australia had adopted this policy and it had been endorsed by the 1911 Imperial Conference. But after Mr Winston Churchill became First Lord of the Admiralty in October 1912, Admiralty policy had altered. The view was then taken that the Japanese Alliance would, for the time being, adequately safeguard Imperial interests in the Pacific and that the real defence of Australia against the likely enemy, Germany, did not rest with an Australian squadron in the Pacific but with the British Battle Fleet in the North Sea. Hence Australia's correct naval policy should be to contribute any capital ships to the British Home Fleet, while only retaining light cruisers in the Pacific for commerce protection. But the Australian Government—whether Labour or Liberal—was strongly opposed to such a change of policy. The Japanese Alliance was felt to be an insecure basis for the protection of Australia in the Pacific, and national pride demanded that Australia's Home Fleet should be a complete one and not merely a light cruiser squadron. On several occasions Denman had spoken in favour of the Australian views and against the policy of contribution to the British Home Fleet by Australia. The question became so controversial that Mr Churchill's speech in Parliament on the Annual Estimates in March 1914, in which he firmly stated the Admiralty's policy, provoked such a storm in Australia that the Australian Parliament published a White Paper in defence of the Australian view.

Whatever the cause of the Home Government's refusal to allow Denman to stay at his post till July, he had to announce his resignation in a speech at Melbourne in January. Writing to his aunt in England, he told her that his dreams of a career were all over. His health and Trudie's dislike of the life, he wrote, had forced him to resign, even if in so doing he offended the Authorities at home. However, he felt that he had earned a few years' retirement after the very heavy strain and he would 'say goodbye to public life and its cares and worries and disappointments'.

Denman's bad health was the official reason given for his resignation. As an Australian newspaper quipped, 'the Governor-

General felt that his was a position that was not to be sneezed at!' The news was received in Australia with general and genuine regret, both the official world and the newspapers uniting in praise of the retiring Governor-General and his wife. Fisher, the Labour ex-Prime Minister, described Denman as 'the best Governor-General they had ever had', and even the very left wing and usually highly critical New South Wales *Worker* praised him as having made friends with Labour and retained their friendship even when Labour was out of office, and said that he would be best remembered as a man who took an intelligent interest in Australian politics. The newspapers' tributes to Trudie were especially sincere and warm. The Sydney *Morning Herald* offered the gratitude of the people of New South Wales 'for her gracious activities in a host of ways, which have aided her husband and made her a popular figure throughout the Commonwealth.' Another paper called her 'the most popular and genuinely liked vice-regal lady we have ever had at Government House'; while the general newspaper comment fastened on her 'unaffectedness, friendliness and sincerity, her keen interest, ready sympathy and quite remarkable business capacity.' Many tributes, too, were paid to her sportsmanship and love of games which counted for so much in Australia.

English newspaper comment on Denman's resignation varied with the political bias of individual papers. The Conservative *Morning Post* was derogatory, and the *Daily Mail*'s statement that 'Lord Denman the evicted of Melbourne (*sic*) was a failure from the first' produced a strong counterblast in Australia, as being typical of the ignorance of the London Press, the leading Melbourne paper declaring that 'the evicted of Sydney was, as a matter of fact, the most successful Governor-General since Lord Tennyson or earlier.'

Amid a barrage of laudatory farewell addresses, the Denmans sailed from Melbourne in the middle of May 1914.

CHAPTER VI

1914–1918

The Denmans were still on board ship when they heard the news of the murder of the Austrian Archduke at Serajevo, and they did not reach England until just before war began. Their London home at 4 Buckingham Gate awaited their arrival, but Balcombe Place was let until 1916. For the first two summer holidays Trudie rented houses in Surrey, after which she occupied Stonehall, the old house on the Balcombe estate where the Grants had lived before they went to Kenya. As soon as Trudie was home, her father wrote to her asking her to resume responsibility for the management of the Balcombe estate.

When, in August, war was declared, Denman went off to camp at Bognor, in command of a regiment of the County of London (Middlesex) Yeomanry, while Trudie became the moving spirit in a war charity called the 'Smokes for Wounded Soldiers and Sailors Society'. The 'S.S.S.', as the Society was commonly called, had Queen Alexandra as its patron, and an impressive Committee headed by Field-Marshal Lord Grenfell and Admiral Lord Charles Beresford, with wives of leading admirals and generals amongst its members. The Society operated from 4 Buckingham Gate, where Trudie turned the ballroom into a packing room. The house was soon crammed with cigarettes and packers. The S.S.S. voluntary workers met all hospital ships and trains and supplied all the Service hospitals with much-appreciated free smokes. Trudie became the Society's Chairman in 1916, and by the time she resigned in 1917 under pressure of other work, close on £67,000 had been raised in subscriptions. Overheads being negligible, 265 million cigarettes had been distributed as well as large quantities of tobacco, pipes and cigars.

Trudie threw herself into the work of the S.S.S. to help her forget her difficulties with her husband which had come to a head. As she wrote to him, their marriage had brought little happiness to either of them; she always seemed inadvertently to be offending him in some way or another, and the atmosphere of living in disgrace had a terribly depressing effect on her. She went on to say that she did not feel that they would ever really understand each other and find the happiness that mutual sympathy and reliance should bring. But Trudie had promised her father and mother not to do anything in haste, and Denman, his pride deeply wounded, pleaded against any permanent separation.

Trudie also had to find relief in her work from the shock of the death of her youngest brother Geoffrey, one of the war's first casualties. He had volunteered as a motor-cycle despatch rider and was captured by a party of Uhlans on the first day of the Battle of the Marne. Three days later he tried to escape when his guards were attacked by the French, but was seen and shot. He left a widow and a three-year-old daughter.

Harold, the eldest Pearson son, was a major in the Sussex Yeomanry, and Trudie was soon to endure much anxious suspense when, in 1915, he went with his regiment to Gallipoli. On those beaches early in May died the member of Denman's staff in Australia whose admiration and friendship for Trudie had meant so much to her. The sadness and worry that surrounded her were, however, relieved by the unexpected arrival at Buckingham Gate of her old friend Nellie Grant. She and her small daughter had returned from Kenya after her husband had joined the forces. They were given a home at Buckingham Gate, and Nellie's unquenchable vitality and eager zest for life provided just the companionship that Trudie needed. With Nellie she was able to recapture some of the fun that they had enjoyed together in pre-Australia days. Trudie had the capacity to put things out of her mind and concentrate with all her faculties on the job of the moment, and she and Nellie were soon deep in a new joint enterprise. Trudie had conceived the idea that a useful and practical way of making use of waste scraps and saving food imports would be for every possible household to keep poultry. She and Nellie accordingly started a scheme to encourage back-yard hen keeping for everybody. They took an office in Pimlico and commissioned a friend to design a model back-yard hen-house which they then advertised, as well as obtaining publicity by persuading friends and hospitals to install these back-yard units. As a result, their office was flooded with thousands of inquiries about the units and about poultry keeping in general. Nellie Grant had a little practical experience, while Trudie 'mugged up the subject', as she wrote to Denman. Between them, although they had no office staff or organization, they answered all the inquirers. They particularly enjoyed tendering advice to poultry keepers of longstanding. Trudie's new enthusiasm also led her to attend a poultry conference and lectures at Cowdray. She started a poultry farm of her own at Balcombe and began to form plans for a cooperative poultry colony of smallholders at Balcombe after the war. This, however, never materialized.

That autumn (1915) Trudie finally made up her mind not to break up her marriage. A very cheering family event was the wedding of her brother Clive, who had been seconded to help his father in the vitally important work of securing oil supplies for the allied navies. He married Trudie's close friend Alicia Knatchbull-Hugessen, whom Trudie had taken to Australia in 1913. But next year (1916) she lost her partner in the poultry enterprise when Mrs Grant went to Spain to join her husband who had been made one of the military attachés in Madrid. By this time, however, Trudie was acquiring a new interest and was starting her connection with the movement in which she was to find her greatest opportunity of service to women and with which her name will always be associated.

Nineteen years earlier the first Women's Institute had been founded by a group of farm women in Canada. The movement spread, encouraged by the Provincial Governments who recognized its great social, educational and economic value. Belgium, Poland and the U.S.A. subsequently followed Canada's lead. In England and Wales the Agricultural Organization Society (to be referred to henceforth as the A.O.S. by which abbreviation it was generally known) had been formed in 1901 with the object of starting local societies of farmers and smallholders for co-operative and other purposes. But although the plea had been made (first in a book published in 1904 and, again, in 1912 in a Report to the

Board of Education) that the A.O.S. should inaugurate Women's Institutes on the Canadian and Belgian models, the Society had got no further than experimenting with introducing women members into local Farm Co-operatives. The experiment had proved a complete failure, the women taking no part in business or discussions for fear of being made fun of by the men. The women of rural England and Wales formed, indeed, the most neglected section of the nation. Spiritually, the blight on village life was its narrowness of outlook, with the women's horizons bounded by the never-ending toil of bringing up large families on miserably low wages in primitive homes. The little that was done to enlarge village women's lives was not done for the women as a whole, but only for those who belonged to a particular Church or political party. Materially, the villages had not shared in the great progress made in the cities and towns in the past fifty years. About 1880 the imports of cheap corn and meat from overseas had ended the golden age of British agriculture. In the twenty dark years that followed, capital ceased to be spent on improvements in land buildings and equipment, while landlords and tenants were forced to neglect the repairs needed to prevent the growing dilapidation of farms and cottages. The skills of the rural craftsmen—the masons, bricklayers, carpenters, woodsmen and blacksmiths—were no longer in demand. Although a measure of prosperity returned to farming with the new century, farm workers' wages remained very low, and village homes obtained none of the modern amenities that had reached the townswomen. Small wonder that the most gifted younger men and women migrated to the towns where even unskilled wages were half as high again as the wages of agricultural workers, while the earnings of the artisans were twice as high. So long as an unfailing supply of cheap imported food formed the basis of the expanding national economy, Governments were content to leave British agriculture to work out its own salvation. Nor did they fear that such growing reliance on external food supplies would endanger the country in time of war. Had not a Royal Commission reported in 1903 that there was 'no reasonable probability of serious interference with supplies'? But 1914 had brought an unexpected menace in the shape of the submarine blockade, and the home farms soon began to assume a new importance. In February 1915 the subject of agricultural co-operation was discussed at a conference in London, opened by Mr Nugent Harris, the Secretary of the A.O.S. Towards the close of the meeting it was addressed by a Canadian, Mrs Alfred Watt, who had been one of those responsible for the success of the Women's Institute movement in Canada. On her husband's death in 1913, she had come to England to educate her two sons and in the hope that she might help to start a Women's Institute movement here. Her efforts had met with no success, but now she secured the invaluable and determined support of Mr Nugent Harris. With considerable difficulty he succeeded in persuading the A.O.S. to assume the responsibility of starting Women's Institutes in England and Wales. Mrs Watt was appointed organizer. The first success was in Wales. Thanks to the local influence of Colonel Stapleton Cotton, one of the Governors of the A.O.S., the first Women's Institute was formed in September 1915 in the Anglesey village of Llanfairpwllgwyngyllgognychwymdrobwllllandysiliogogogoch.

By Christmas 1915 three more Institutes had been formed in Wales and three in England, while a Women's Institute Sub-Committee of the A.O.S. had been appointed to supervise the project. It met in December and adopted model rules for the Institutes which, like their Canadian counterparts, were to be democratic, non-sectarian and non-political. If it was the urgent war-time need to conserve and increase home food supplies that supplied the immediate incentive for founding Women's Institutes, the inspiration and intention of those enthusiasts who started the movement went far beyond such material aims. As in Canada, the Institutes were to be so organized as to fill a permanent need in the life of countrywomen and to work for the general good of the village community. 'We, the members of the Llanfair Women's Institute, pledge ourselves to do our utmost to make the Institute the centre of good in our neighbourhood.' So ran the first resolution of the first Women's Institute.

By the autumn of 1916 the number of Institutes had risen to

twenty-four, and Mrs Nugent Harris had come to the A.O.S. as Honorary Secretary to the Women's Institute Sub-Committee. More members had been appointed to it, and the need of a permanent Chairman was felt. This appointment was the main business of the Sub-Committee's third meeting on October 3rd, 1916, when it was resolved to recommend to the A.O.S. that Lady Salisbury should be asked to become Chairman. Failing her acceptance, the name of Lady Denman was put forward.

Mrs Roland Wilkins (née Louisa Jebb) was the Governor of the A.O.S. who pressed Lady Denman's qualifications for the post. She was acting as Chairman of the Sub-Committee but was anxious to resign, since she was opposed to the Women's Institute movement being sponsored and organized by the A.O.S. Instead, she believed firmly that the Institutes should be an autonomous woman's movement, completely rural in character and directed especially towards the cottagers. Mrs Wilkins had probably met Lady Denman in connection with her poultry activities and plans for Balcombe smallholdings. At any rate she had been impressed by Trudie's practical and unsentimental outlook, and had also found in her someone whose belief in the right and ability of women to conduct their own affairs was as sound as her own; someone moreover who had been trained in methods of procedure and administration in the hard school of the Women's Liberal Federation, and who, in Australia, had not only become familiar with public life but who had also there shown her special interest in countrywomen. Mrs Wilkins may well have also felt that Lady Denman's title and position would help to gain the support of the 'county' to the new movement.

Lady Salisbury refused the post, but Trudie accepted and was at once made a Governor of the A.O.S. She admired Mrs Wilkins and saw in the proposal an opportunity—although neither she nor anyone else could then guess how great a one—to forget her own troubles in devoting herself to work for which her background and experience seemed to fit her and which made a special appeal to the deep sense of fair play and justice that lay at the core of her being. As in the Australian outback, it was in the villages of

Britain that the lot of women was hardest and most repressed. Only privately, inside the home, were the women able to exercise their influence; outside, their apathy and indifference and their fear of ridicule or of offending 'their betters' left men to do the talking and the organizing. Hardly a breath of the movement for women's freedom and equality had reached the countryside, where women still had no voice in the affairs of the community and possessed no outside interests in which—as Trudie was doing —to escape from and put into perspective the brooding cares of home life.

Although Trudie was still Chairman of the 'Smokes', and had also become President of the Women's section of the Poultry Association, she threw herself wholeheartedly into the new work. By the beginning of 1917 forty Institutes had been formed and more were coming into being each month. The problem at head-quarters was how to finance the rapidly-expanding demand for the formation of new Institutes and to obtain more organizers to relieve the overburdened Mrs Watt. It was decided that the A.O.S. must be asked to demand an increased vote from the Treasury in order to pay for four salaried organizers. But this request enhanced the doubts of the A.O.S. as to the propriety of their continuing to assume responsibility for a movement whose rapid growth would inevitably deflect the attention of the A.O.S. from the work of promoting agricultural co-operation for which it had been constituted. The Treasury took a similar view, and in September (1917) Lady Denman and her sub-committee were summoned to an emergency meeting to hear the news that finance for the required organizers could not be provided by the A.O.S. Instead, the proposal was made that the administration of the Institutes should be taken over by the Women's Branch of the Board of Agriculture's Food Department. This was a new Branch which had been set up to form a Woman's Land Army so as to provide a mobile force of workers who would go anywhere and supplement the local and sporadic part-time work of women on the land. The need for such an army was urgent. As Mr Prothero, the Minister of Agriculture, told Miss (later Dame) Meriel Talbot whom he appointed Director of the new Branch, 'England is like a beleaguered city.' There was, in fact, only about three weeks' food supply in the country.

The Women's Institute Sub-Committee felt that they had no alternative but to leave the shelter of the A.O.S. Trudie was therefore empowered to negotiate the terms of transfer with the Board of Agriculture. In a broadcast thirty years later Trudie told of that critical moment in the fortunes of the Women's Institutes. Her great concern was to try to preserve the democratic and independent character of the movement from the dead hand of official control. As she walked down Victoria Street for her first discussion with Miss Talbot she was wondering by what possible means the Institutes could become a self-governing organization.

'I didn't know much about Government Departments in those days,' Trudie recalled, 'but I was convinced that country-women were overlooked by the Authorities and that unless they got together to put their case this unhappy state of things would continue. The 140 Institutes scattered through England and Wales were not then a Federation—a few of us had been discussing the need for a proper constitution, but how was I to convince a Government Department that if these village societies were to be controlled by a Ministry or by Local Authorities their value would be nil? I arrived at my interview prepared for battle and ready to spin a yarn that there'd be a riot in the countryside if the Women's Institutes became official organizations. Luckily my truthfulness was not put to the test, for Dame Meriel took it for granted that the Institutes must unite to manage their own affairs. Their formation was thus undertaken by the Food Production Department—that meant that new Institutes were formed by the Government—but after that they became the responsibility of the National Federation; in other words the Institutes themselves laid down policy and made their own rules at the annual general meeting of the Federation, and by these decisions all the Women's Institutes were and are bound. Thus, owing to the understanding and to the lack of red tape of a Government Department of those days, the Women's Institutes became self-governing.'

Such was the broad agreement arrived at between Trudie and Miss Talbot. For its immediate implementation a Women's Institute Section was formed in Miss Talbot's branch of the Board of Agriculture, and, in a letter from the Board dated October 4th, Lady Denman was appointed Honorary Assistant Director to Miss Talbot to take charge of the new Section. Mrs Watt was made Organizer with three full-time salaried assistants. The first task was to form the Institutes into a National Federation with a proper constitution. On October 16th, 1917, 60 out of the 137 Institutes sent delegates to a conference in the Central Hall, Westminster. It was the first of the Women's Institutes Annual Meetings. Trudie was elected to the Chair and, after some discussion, the delegates voted unanimously in favour of the transfer of the Institutes from the A.O.S. to the Board of Agriculture. Trudie then moved the adoption of the draft rules for a constitution, setting up a National Federation under the management of a Committee of eighteen, of whom ten were to be elected by the delegates. After the rules had been unanimously adopted, the delegates elected their representatives on the management committee. Trudie's name headed the list, as it was to do each year for the next thirty years. The new Management Committee met the next day. Choosing Trudie as Chairman, the Committee proceeded to work out rules for County Federations to be affiliated to the National Federation.

Before long, Trudie and the Management Committee acquired a Vice-Chairman in the person of Miss Grace Hadow of Cirencester. Nine years older than Trudie, Grace Hadow was a distinguished scholar who had gained First Class Honours in English at Oxford and had returned there as a don. Recalling in after years the beginnings of a close, happy and lasting partnership that was to give the Women's Institute movement so much of its future aims and purposes, Trudie, always conscious of her own academic shortcomings, wrote characteristically that she

'could not believe that anyone of Miss Hadow's knowledge could give such serious consideration to the views of anyone as ignorant as myself. I never really got used to Miss Hadow's humility of mind, and during our long years of association I was impressed by the way in which she received suggestions from us all. She allowed committees to alter the wording of leaflets she had written and letters she had drafted, and never once implied that her command of the English language was greater than that of any of us. I do not think that she herself ever realized or appreciated that she had unique gifts both as a speaker and a writer.'

Nineteen-eighteen was a year of great progress for the Women's Institute movement. Five hundred and seventy-four new Institutes were formed making a total of 760 at the end of the year. But it was also a difficult year for the Management Committee under Trudie's leadership. The system whereby one body, the Board of Agriculture, formed Institutes, and another body, the National Federation, then administered them presented its own problems. Local branches always tend to mistrust Headquarters in any organization and such mistrust is likely to be intensified when the local branches are set up by a different body. Moreover, the voluntary County organizers, appointed and trained by the Board of Agriculture for propaganda and Institute formation, had no direct allegiance to the National Federation. Such division of responsibility could only be resolved by firmness combined with great tact and patience on the part of Trudie and her colleagues on the Management Committee. Trudie later recounted how

'at an early meeting of the Committee I was absent and Miss Hadow took the chair. Unfortunately the meeting spent its time in reviewing the work done in forming new Institutes and making plans for the future. At the following meeting I very nervously had to explain that most of the decisions arrived at at the previous meeting were out of order. I can remember now my very great relief when Miss Hadow took this to be a most comic incident. She often referred to it, and years later would pretend to be relieved when she had been in the chair at a meeting that it had not been necessary to scrap everything that had been decided under her chairmanship.'

As the Management Committee cautiously felt its way forward, it became clear that the rules of the National Constitution would have to be redrafted for submission to the next Annual General meeting. This redrafting occupied much of the Committee's time. There were also other problems. Finance was one. The National Federation's only certain source of income came from the affiliation fee of 2d. per Institute member, of which 1½d. went to the County and only ½d. to the National Federation. Miss Alice Williams, the Management Committee's honorary Treasurer, gave the Federation all the royalties on her patriotic play *Britannia* and undertook to organize an exhibition and sale of work at the Annual General meeting, but application had to be made to the Government for help. As a result, the Treasury gave the Federation £2,000 in the current financial year. The Carnegie United Kingdom Trust also gave £1,000 to help the Institutes establish rural industries. Thus financially reinforced, the Management Committee were able to appoint a paid Secretary and two whole-time organizers.

Another problem arose from the resolution of a Cabinet Reconstruction Committee in favour of mixed village Clubs of men and women, for whose promotion a Village Clubs Association was formed. Trudie was firmly opposed to the Institutes' joining such mixed Clubs. Yet another problem arose over the wish of some towns to start Women's Institutes. Should the movement be thus urbanized or should it retain its strictly rural character? The Management Committee worked out a compromise, but the question was not to be finally settled until ten years later when the National Union of Townswomen's Guilds was formed.

The second Annual General Meeting was held in October 1918 in the Central Hall, Westminster, with Trudie in the Chair. It was a much livelier occasion than the first meeting. Over 500 delegates attended, 'probably the largest meeting of purely rural women ever held in London' Trudie said in her opening speech. The new Constitutional rules drafted by the Management Committee were adopted after much animated discussion. The preamble firmly defined the movement's aims.

'The Women's Institute Movement,' it ran, 'was started to provide means for the effective development of the part countrywomen can play in rural development by supplying an organization in country districts through which an educational policy can be given full effect, and by which the knowledge gained can be applied practically in the different branches of agriculture, rural industries, domestic science, hygiene and social welfare.'

One important alteration was made to the rules for the individual Institutes. Their character was now defined as 'non-party' instead of as 'non-political'. This was to meet the eagerness of the Institutes, which Trudie fully shared, for the movement to be free to take political, as distinct from party-political, action on public questions affecting village women. As a first result, the delegates pledged the Institutes to press their Local Authority fully to implement the Government's state-aided housing scheme. After considerable discussion on the question of mixed Village Clubs, the meeting agreed that any action to alter the constitution of Women's Institutes was to be deprecated.

The next day, the Exhibition of Institute work, including exhibits of handicrafts, garden produce and small livestock, was held in the Caxton Hall. Opened by Mrs Lloyd George and visited by the Queen and Princess Mary, it was a great success, in spite of an unfortunate incident when a number of rabbits broke loose and had to be chased round the hall by members of the Management Committee just as Trudie was about to receive the royal guests!

The Annual Meeting endorsed an increase in the elected members of the Management Committee (henceforth to be called the Executive Committee) from ten to fifteen, and elected the new membership by secret ballot; Trudie and Miss Williams heading the poll. It was already apparent to all the delegates that in Lady Denman the Women's Institutes had not only found a Chairman with the gift of handling a large meeting with exceptional competence, but that under her leadership over the past two war-time years, the movement had made sound and striking progress. It was with confidence that they looked to their future in times of peace.

Meantime Trudie had anticipated the fashion that was to come into vogue after the war by having her lovely long hair cut short. The cause of this was an attack of typhoid fever at the end of 1917. 'Typhoid was well worth it,' was Trudie's comment. She had always resented the waste of time in doing up long hair.

In addition to her Chairmanship of the Women's Institute Management Committee, Trudie's position under Miss Talbot at the Board of Agriculture involved her in general headquarters work for the Women's Land Army. Her friend Nellie Grant now came back on the scene. She had returned from Spain in 1917 and was given a Land Army organizing job first in Dorset and then at Winchester. Together, Trudie and she took part in a great Land Army recruiting drive in 1918. There was, of course, no wireless through which to make appeals, and open-air rallies were the chosen medium for recruiting. Dressed in Land Army uniforms, Trudie and Nellie drove round the Southern Counties in a small car and hugely enjoyed themselves. Stopping the car in the middle of the High Street or in the Market Place of the towns, one of them would attract the public's startled attention by rotating a policeman's very heavy wooden alarm rattle, which made an ear-splitting noise. After this, the other would make a rousing recruiting speech standing on the step of the car. Sometimes they were invited to use the stage of theatres or cinemas, and once, in Portsmouth, they followed a turn by performing dogs and had a riotous reception from a sailor audience. At Southampton they joined a parade with the Wrens and Waacs. Finding that a seven-mile march through the streets was involved, they hired horses from a livery stable and formed the only mounted element in the procession, refuting the protests of the organizers by insisting that horses were indubitably agricultural! Their only trouble was that when they occasionally stayed with friends in large and smart houses, they were apt to find that they had just signed on their friends' last remaining parlourmaid or housemaid. Once, however, when they were performing with their rattle in Guildford High Street, Trudie suddenly seized Nellie and dragged her into a shop. The cause was a huge yellow Rolls-Royce that swept by with liveried chauffeur. Seated inside the car was Lady Cowdray! Her daughter's undignified performance would *not* have met with her approval.

CHAPTER VII

The Women's Institutes, 1919–1938

(i)

In 1919, peacetime prospects for agriculture and for the villages of Britain seemed rosier than they had been for forty years. The farmers, with guaranteed prices for wheat and oats, had greatly increased production during the war. Prosperity had returned to the countryside. Moreover, this time, the farm worker's increased wages had given him a share in the new prosperity. Now, Mr Lloyd George, the Prime Minister, was solemnly promising that farming should never again be left unsupported by the State. But the sunshine was short-lived. By the end of 1920 world prices for agricultural produce were already beginning to collapse, and in 1921, regardless of promises, the Government's guarantees both for farmers' prices and for farm workers' wages were withdrawn. No longer fearing hunger, Britain seemed to have lost all interest in her home agriculture. Once again the farmer was thrown back on his own resources to compete as best he could in a wholly unprotected market. By the end of 1922 wheat prices had fallen by half, and the price of milk had declined almost as sharply. For the next four years prices continued to fall. Then, after three years of relative stability, came the second world-wide slump in commodity prices. By the middle of 1933 farm prices were back at their pre-war level, and each £1,000 that a farmer had invested in his business in 1920 was worth only £250. The farm labourer's wage had, however, been protected by the 1924 Agricultural Wages Act, so that in 1933 it was still at about the same level as in 1922. But the gap between wages on the farm and those obtainable in the towns was as great as ever, and even the existing rate of farm wages was so high in relation to farm prices that a reduction in his labour bill became the farmer's paramount consideration. Four million acres of arable land were therefore put down to grass, and the number of agricultural workers declined by thirty per cent, chiefly among the younger men. After prices had reached their lowest, State assistance began to be given in one form or another to most kinds of agricultural produce; and, as the threat of a new war revived the spectre of national hunger, this assistance was increased. Nevertheless the general atmosphere of the countryside between the wars was one of defeat and depression, with farms impoverished and neglected, cottages and buildings falling into disrepair, and with most villages still lacking the amenities that were now taken for granted in the towns.

It is the more remarkable that it was in this period of acute depression and against this general background of rural decay, that the Women's Institute movement grew year by year in numbers, vitality, and effective influence. At the end of 1918 there were 760 Institutes; by the beginning of 1928 4,000 villages had their Institute, and the movement had become the voice of a quarter of a million countrywomen. By 1938 the number of Institutes had risen to over 5,500, with a total membership of more than 350,000. Overcoming agelong apathy and self-distrust, the countrywomen of England and Wales met each month in their Institutes to gain not only wider horizons and new practical skills for self-expression, but also, through their Institutes' democratic procedure, to learn citizenship and the duty of taking a lively interest in local and national affairs in order to fulfil the first resolution of the first Women's Institute—to make their Institute a 'centre of good' for its neighbourhood.

The changes that have come about in the English countryside since 1919 are revolutionary. Thought and expression in the villages are no longer dominated by the squire and parson; recreational facilities no longer lag far behind those in the towns, to which improved transport gives an access formerly unknown; electricity, piped water, sewerage, the telephone, the extension of medical and nursing services have brought the countrywoman the amenities enjoyed by the townswoman and have relieved her of much of the drudgery of her life; and the countrywoman herself has become a real force in local affairs and local Government. Directly and indirectly the influence of the Women's Institutes in bringing about these changes has been immense. From the movement's very early days until 1946 this influence was inspired and directed by Trudie Denman as Chairman of the National Federation and active head of the whole movement.

The year 1937 marked the Institutes' 21st birthday. At their Annual General Meeting in the Albert Hall, attended by over 5,000 delegates, Lady Denman was presented with a commemorative Institute book. It became one of her most treasured possessions and is now treasured by her daughter. Each county in England and Wales was responsible for producing a page, inscribed with the names of its Institutes and distinctively illustrating the county's special activities and beauties. In the skill of their design and execution the pages resemble an illustrated mediaeval manuscript. The book was dedicated to 'Lady Denman, in token that there is no county in England and Wales in which her name is not held in warm affection and respect as that of a wise and just Chairman and a true friend, and in grateful recognition and acknowledgement of 21 years of unsparing service to Women's Institutes.'

(ii)

What were the special directions in which Trudie Denman's inspiration and leadership most influenced the Institute movement? In her speech at the 1937 Annual General Meeting and in her broadcast to the 350,000 Institute members that followed it, she herself made her own views clear.

'To my mind,' she said in her broadcast, 'the greatest achievement of the Institutes is that we have learned to govern ourselves. We do not believe in dictators; we believe that each member should be responsible for her Institute and should have a share in the work. It may be as a member of Committee; it may be as one of those responsible for the entertainment; it may be as a helper at tea; or as a steward arranging the meeting; but the many jobs that have to be done in the perfect Women's Institute are shared by the members and are not undertaken by one or two super-women.'

And in her speech at the Meeting, she put first of the achievements that 'in our movement we enjoy liberty and democratic government. The smallest of the W.I.s can move a resolution at this great meeting, and if that resolution is carried it becomes the policy of us all.'

Trudie's most firmly held belief was her faith in human nature and in democracy. From the outset she was determined to build up a completely democratic and independent organization of countrywomen in which the ordinary village woman and not just the county lady should have a voice and a platform. She felt that a soundly-based constitution for the Movement was the first essential to this end. Here, Trudie's experience with the Women's Liberal Federation was of great service to her, and her ideas were largely based on the constitution of that body as set up by the Countess of Carlisle. During 1919 much of the Executive Committee's time was occupied with the general question of how the Movement should be governed, particularly in respect of the relationship between the County Federations and National Headquarters. Under Trudie's guidance, it was finally decided that the National Executive should continue to be annually elected by the direct votes of the Institutes, but that an advisory Consultative Council should also be formed, composed of County representatives. The decision was the more important, since the Board of Agriculture had given notice that it intended forthwith to hand over to the National Federation its responsibilities for propaganda and Institute formation work. Some counties were loath to lose the shelter of a Government Department, but Trudie welcomed the Movement's complete administrative independence.

Essential to the future well-being of the Movement as was the right solution of its constitution, Trudie also realized that the democratic nature of the individual Institutes and of the County and National Federations could only be preserved if proper rules of procedure for all Institute meetings were drawn up and were understood by all members. Above all, she was insistent on a secret ballot each year in each Institute for the election of its Officers and Committee. It was only, she felt, by strictly following the rules of procedure that petty squabbles could be avoided and the ordinary village woman member protected from domination in her Institute by 'county' snobbery or Committee careerists. This was a very real danger since the squires' and parsons' wives were still ruling forces in most villages, and in the eyes of many of them the idea that the cottager was entitled to an equal voice with theirs smacked of Bolshevism. In one Somerset village, where the lady of the manor was Chairman of the Institute and had also built the Village Hall where the Institute held its monthly meeting, the Institute's Committee had the temerity to decide a point against the lady's wishes. When next the Institute members went to the Village Hall to hold their meeting, they found the door screwed up to bar their entry. On the advice of Headquarters in London, the members met instead in each other's kitchens. The Institute became a notably flourishing one.

It was not, therefore, from any love of procedure and rules for their own sake that Trudie set such importance on them. She worked hard to achieve her own mastery of public procedure. She herself wrote a pamphlet for Institute guidance on the subject, and inspired the production of the National Federation handbook, as well as leaflets on the duties of Secretaries and specimen accounts and minutes books—all models of clear and easily understood English. She also convened and herself conducted training courses for Institute officers all over the country. As Trudie said at one such conference, 'It is better for a meeting to make the wrong decision it wishes to make than the right decision which its Chairman wishes it to make.'

Another aspect of the Institutes' organization that was always uppermost in Trudie's mind was also referred to in her speech at the 21st Annual General Meeting.

'Are we satisfied,' she said, 'that we are using the youth within our ranks to the fullest advantage? Are we sure that we have the enthusiasm and enterprise which are the attributes of youth and that those younger than ourselves are ready to step into our shoes? Above all, do we remember that the real appeal to youth is the opportunity for service and sacrifice?'

Apart from questions of organization, one particularly difficult and critical constitutional issue reared its head from time to time. This was the preservation of the completely non-sectarian and non-party-political character of the Movement. Trudie regarded it as vital. As the Institutes grew in number and reputation they offered a most attractive platform for propagandist organizations, and the Executive had to remain ever watchful to prevent the Institutes being exploited for party-political or sectarian causes. On the other hand, as Trudie fully realized, there was the very real risk that the easy course of forbidding discussion of any big issues would result in the Institutes becoming mere entertainment centres or technical schools for farmers' wives, instead of the force for social reform which Trudie so ardently desired them to be. In a statement which she made at a consultative Conference in 1935 she laid down the principles which she felt the Institutes should follow in this dilemma.

'We are all of us,' she said, 'at some time faced with the problem of what or may not be discussed at W.I. meetings, at County Federation meetings and at the Annual General Meeting. . . . In the first place, we must, I think, accept the fact that almost every question is, or may become in one or other of its aspects, either party-political or sectarian. Take for example the subjects of malnutrition, maternal mortality and agriculture, all vital matters which it is important for Institutes to study and discuss; but malnutrition might easily raise the party question of the amount of public assistance, maternal mortality might raise the sectarian problem of birth control, and agriculture might involve the party question of subsidies. . . . It may be argued that it is better not to discuss at all anything that cannot be studied in all its aspects, but this principle, carried to its logical conclusion, would, I think, exclude discussion on almost every vital question of the day. If it were accepted by the Institutes it would debar them from carrying out much of their most important educational work, would lessen both their influence and the value of that influence in national affairs and would turn them into social clubs with no activities of general interest and importance. My own opinion is that emphasis should lie, not on the avoidance of all subjects that might give rise to party-political or sectarian points, but on the conduct of all discussions within limits which will not cause any infringement of our rule in this matter; and I do not think it is beyond our capacity to make a decision as to these limits in the discussion of any particular subject. . . . We must all take the responsibility of ensuring that our non-party and non-sectarian rules are kept. This is no easy task and will only be successfully accomplished if each subject is considered on its merits and the question approached from a detached point of view. If we shirk this difficult task and discourage W.I.s from discussing anything that might lead to difficulties, I believe that we shall limit ourselves to trivialities and so do irreparable harm to our movement.'

The non-sectarian issue provided Trudie with many fights. She was determined that Church and Chapel should be able to come together in the Institutes—this was especially important in Wales—and her uncompromising attitude earned her a good deal of unpopularity since it appeared to some to stamp her as an agnostic and hostile to religion. In many villages there were men and women who were deeply shocked at what they considered to be the irreligious nature of the Institutes; they strongly opposed the formation of one in their village, and some men refused to allow their wives to join it when formed. Trudie made her own position clear in the course of a discussion on the movement of the Churches to ensure that more religious instruction was given in the schools.

'Can W.I. members forward this movement?' she asked. 'The answer is as individuals or as a member of a Church, "Yes"; as a W.I. member, "No". The W.I.s can and should uphold the supreme importance of spiritual values, but people of widely varying views may join an Institute and it would be against the fundamental principles of Institute membership to ask them to join in a demand for religious instruction with which they may not agree. Let us concentrate on furthering the Christian virtues of Charity, Truth, Unselfishness and Justice, and try to get religious teaching for children through the Churches and not through the Institute.'

And, in a letter which she sent to all members of the Executive Committee, she wrote,

'It has been stated that since all the Churches are now agreed on certain principles, sectarian strife need not arise. . . but such a measure of agreement does not materially affect the situation since people themselves do not agree—to one woman religion may mean worship, prayer and high ideals, to the next it is "no games on Sunday", and to the third it is the Parson trying to make her go to the Church. It is an evasion to pretend that religion and religious education can be discussed without the inevitable ultimate discussion of what religion, what religious education? . . . and there is nothing which is more potentially dangerous to one's love of one's neighbour.'

Difficulties over the party-political issue came to a head in 1934. From 1919, the Executive Committee with Trudie's full support had encouraged Institutes to join the League of Nations Union so as to make common cause with women all over the world in efforts for the peaceful settlement of international disputes through the League. But when, in 1934, the Executive Committee refused to allow the Navy League to send speakers to address Institutes, Lord Lloyd, the Navy League's Chairman, in an interview with Lady Denman, accused the Institutes of being a 'pacifist' body. The letter that Trudie addressed to all County Federations affords another example of her fine and courageous leadership.

'A number of groups and Institutes have been having speakers from the Navy League,' she wrote. 'Recently, however, there have been complaints that a speaker from the Navy League has been attacking pacifists and urging W.I. members to leave the League of Nations Union and join the Navy League instead. It is, of course, open to any W.I. to have a discussion on the League of Nations, and the fact that our Annual Meeting has several times passed resolutions in favour of the principles for which it stands does not prevent us from criticizing the League or from changing our minds if we so desire. But to use a W.I.

Balcombe Place

meeting for an attack on pacifism is to infringe the rule which forbids us to touch on party-political or sectarian ground. Many of our members belong to religious bodies which hold that to resist by force is morally wrong. We may agree or disagree with the religious belief of various of the Churches or Religious Societies which are represented among our members, but our movement accepts members of any Church on the guarantee that at W.I. meetings there shall be nothing which can give them just cause for offence.

'Many Societies exist to advocate particular political or religious beliefs or practices, and anyone who wishes to do so can join them; it is also open to anyone as an individual or as a member of such a society, to organize a meeting to advocate militarism or pacifism or any other view which he or she wishes to bring forward. The Women's Institutes, however, feel that they have ample scope in concentrating on the things which women of all creeds and parties have in common; and to very many members it is a real inspiration to have a movement which is outside all factions.'

(iv)

In her speech at the 1937 Annual General Meeting, Trudie turned to

'the great questions which affect us all.' 'Are we satisfied,' she said, 'that the beauty and value of our land is being preserved? Are we content with conditions of life in the countryside? Are we satisfied that our health services are adequate to our needs; or can ill-health and the disability which exists among women be lessened?'

It was over such questions that Trudie's leadership most inspired the Institute movement. One such subject was rural education, and for thirty years better educational opportunities for village women formed one of the Movement's most important campaigns. A resolution of the Executive Committee testified to Trudie's contribution to this cause. 'Without her enthusiasm, persistence and foresight,' the resolution ran, 'the success which came at last might never have been achieved.'

Early in 1926, at the invitation of the Minister of Education, Trudie began twenty years' service on the Committee for selecting rural boys and girls for Ministry of Agriculture scholarships. Shortly before (in December 1925) she had undertaken the onerous task of Chairmanship of a special Committee set up under the Ministry of Agriculture and the Board of Education to 'consider the general question of the practical education of women for rural life.' No previous attempt had been made to survey this question. In 1928, after meeting seventeen times and interviewing thirty-five witnesses, the Committee issued its report, for which Trudie was largely responsible. In a letter to her daughter, she described how she had stayed in bed and 'spent three hours on the report of the Education Committee, as it didn't seem to me to be concise enough. In fact it was very long-winded, which as you know I like in a letter but not in a document of 50 large pages.' Known as the Denman Report, its contents, which the Authorities considered 'a notable and valuable contribution', covered not only the practical education for rural life of adult country-women, but also that of girls leaving the country schools at 14 and that of the younger girls in the elementary and secondary schools. Fundamental to the whole report was the concept that village women make a unique and twofold contribution to agriculture; the 'independent' contribution of women farmers and paid workers (of whom there were over 100,000 in 1926); and the 'co-operative' contribution made by a very much larger number of women and girls by virtue of their position as wives or daughters in village homes, where they are far more intimately associated with and have a far greater influence on the work of their menfolk than is the case in other industries. Practical education for women in rural life must therefore embrace not only the growing of produce in the field and garden, but also its subsequent utilization in the kitchen, and instruction in home management and crafts.

Following up her report, Trudie headed deputations from the Institutes' Executive Committee to the Minister of Agriculture and to the President of the Board of Education. Reporting to the 1930 Annual General Meeting, she told the delegates that Mr Noel

Buxton, the Minister of Agriculture, had received her most sympathetically, and that he was obtaining a special grant for training teachers in farm household management, as well as appointing more women inspectors to advise the County Authorities on the education of women in agricultural subjects. By the end of 1930 the first of these new teachers was already at work, and rural domestic economy had been officially recognized as a branch of agricultural education.

In January of 1930 Trudie also gave the introductory broadcast to a series of technical talks for countrywomen arranged by the B.B.C. After reminding her hearers of the countrywoman's need for expert advice and training on subjects ranging from dairying and poultry keeping to first-aid in the home, she went on to tell them of the responsibility of their local authorities for giving them such help.

> 'Now I should like to remind you,' she said, 'that it is part of the duties of the County Councils to teach cooking to country girls and women. But, as a matter of fact, of girls in the country elementary schools, only thirty-one in every hundred get this teaching and as for adult women, in many counties they get no classes at all.'

Village water supplies and the disposal of refuse were other matters which she urged them to take up with their local authorities.

> 'It is difficult,' she said, 'in the country to get rid of old tins and so on. But these *can* be collected if you really persuade your local authorities that you want it done. I also wish that those of you who live in a village where the water has to be carried from a well which dries up in the summer, and at the best of times produces not very pure water, would get together and find out what your local authority can do to help you.'

She ended by asking her audience

> 'to remember the parable in St Luke's gospel of the widow who came to the judge saying "avenge me of mine adversary. And

he would not for a while". But, afterwards, he said, "Yet, because this widow troubleth me I will avenge her lest by her continual coming she weary me." Now you see that was the point of view 2,000 years ago; and women had no vote then. I believe that now (not particularly widows) but all country-women, especially if they are Institute members, could get much more help than they do at present if they remembered this parable and, of course, acted accordingly.'

(v)

Trudie also never ceased to give a lead to the Institute Movement over rural health services. One aspect was the provision of clean, safe milk and its free or cheap distribution to schools and small children and expectant mothers, reforms which were finally all fully adopted during the Second World War. At the 1938 Annual General Meeting Trudie reported on how she had asked Institutes to write to their Members of Parliament on this subject, and how, when she went to the House of Commons to address a group of members, she found that every member was carrying a large bundle of letters.

'One M.P.,' she said, 'suggested that he would have been saved a lot of work if he had received one letter from the County Federation rather than fifty from individual Institutes. I suggested, in reply, that it was always possible for one letter to be overlooked, whereas fifty were bound to receive attention. Judging by the way I was greeted by a chorus of "Hear, Hears" and laughter, the M.P.'s entirely agreed that there is strength in a united attack.'

Another health aspect to which the Institutes turned their attention in the nineteen thirties was that of nutrition. A special conference was held in London, courses were organized and a quarterly bulletin published on cookery and food values, while in the county of Durham, where unemployment was particularly bad, the Institutes ran nutrition and cookery classes in nearly a hundred villages at the Government's request. The preservation of fruit and vegetables was also taught in all counties, and Trudie encouraged the co-operative marketing of Institute members' produce. As a member of the Carnegie United Kingdom Trust she was instrumental in obtaining a grant by means of which the National Federation was able to appoint a full-time market organizer.

The health of country schoolchildren was yet another subject for resolutions at Annual General Meetings, and the Institutes were asked to exert pressure on local authorities over such matters as school meals, rooms for changing wet footwear and school transport. Another Institute health campaign in which Trudie fought with all her vigour was to make available to village women the facilities such as improved midwifery services and prenatal and infant welfare clinics which had so notably reduced the maternal mortality rates in the cities. Shortly before the outbreak of the Second World War Trudie also made the availability of the new methods of analgesia an object of her deep concern, fighting the medical red tape that debarred village women from their use by ruling that analgesics could only be administered in the presence of two midwives.

Besides rural education and health, Trudie's speeches at the Annual General Meetings made constant reference to campaigns for community objects such as piped water supplies to village homes, cheap electricity for rural areas, telephone boxes in villages, the secret ballot for parish council elections, proper facilities for the collection and destruction of refuse, the preservation of the beauty of the countryside and its ancient buildings, footpaths and wild flowers and for its protection against litter.

Full success in the long-drawn-out battle to achieve all these aims did not come until after the end of the Second World War, but, in their pursuit between the two wars, Trudie gave unsparingly of her time and influence, heading deputations to Members of Parliament, writing to and interviewing Ministers and always encouraging the County Federations never to relax their pressure on their local authorities.

(vi)

Trudie fully recognized the importance of the cultural side of the Institute movement. Indeed, in her speech at the 1937 Annual General Meeting she said 'Foremost, Women's Institutes have, I think, added to the happiness of countrywomen. Through the Institutes the love of acting, of dancing, of singing and of craft work has been aroused and given an opportunity of expression.' But this side of the movement made less personal appeal to Trudie than did questions of organization, education and social reform. She had no special talent for music or drama, and did not herself share in the countrywoman's usual handicrafts such as sewing and embroidery. But if the arts played a minor role in her own life she was keen to encourage talent, and her own activities as a collector showed her ability to recognize genuine quality. In the Institute Movement, with the strong organization that she had built up, she was able to leave the direction and encouragement of the cultural side in what she felt were better and more capable and understanding hands than her own, such as those of Miss Nancy Tennant and other talented Institute leaders. When, however, she became a member of the Carnegie United Kingdom Trust and of its music and drama committee, she was able to negotiate considerable financial help to the Institutes' work in these fields. A note written some years after she had given up the Chairmanship is perhaps typical of her.

'When the National Federation was very young,' she wrote, 'it seemed to some of us that a competition for an Institute song might produce a good but unknown poetess. Miss Hadow took the view that poetry written for a special purpose was unlikely to be good—but still I hoped. Eventually a verse arrived which started with the line, "We are a band of earnest women". This was too much for me, and, as usual, I realized how right Miss Hadow was—hence "Jerusalem" became and remains the W.I. song.'

Blake's 'Jerusalem' with its superb setting by Sir Hubert Parry was, in fact, first sung at the Annual General Meeting of 1924, on the idea of Mr W. H. Leslie, the distinguished amateur of music who played a prominent part in encouraging and directing the Institutes' musical activities.

Throughout these years Trudie had the supreme advantage of the support of a most able team of women at the National Federation Headquarters. There was Grace Hadow, the deputy Chairman, the value of whose brilliant brain was enhanced by the detached point of view which she brought to the consideration of all questions, and by her certainty that no one could be self-seeking. While Trudie and Grace Hadow were one in their belief in democracy, social reform and the rights and capabilities of women, each contributed qualities that were complementary to the other's.

Then there was Mrs Helena Auerbach, until 1927 the movement's Honorary Treasurer. Trudie had the greatest admiration for her 'clear brain and fighting spirit'. Like Trudie and Grace Hadow, Helena Auerbach had been deeply interested in the Women's Suffrage Movement. She had been Honorary Treasurer of the National Union of Women's Suffrage Societies and brought that training and experience to the service of the Institutes. The movement had need of her acumen and practical wisdom in the difficult early days of its finances. When in 1919 the Institutes achieved their administrative independence, the National Federation was still almost wholly financially dependent on a general purposes grant from the Government. Trudie, from the outset, was determined that the movement should achieve financial independence as early as possible. The first step, she felt, was the creation of a capital reserve in the shape of an Endowment Fund; and, in 1920, she promised to give £5,000 to start the fund if the Institutes raised a similar sum within a year. Mrs Auerbach threw herself into raising the money, and by the end of the year £6,600 had been collected, enabling Trudie's gift to be claimed. Next came the need to establish a self-supporting income basis. Aided by the rapid increase in the number of Institutes, and under Mrs Auerbach's shrewd guidance, the movement became progressively able to stand on its own financial feet, until in 1927 the Treasury grant disappeared altogether.

At headquarters, too, Trudie had behind her a strong Executive Committee, elected annually by the direct votes of the Institutes and representative of all parts of the country. At first, National Federation headquarters was housed in a small, dark and inconvenient flat in a large block in Victoria Street. The Executive Committee used to lunch together between sessions at the Army and Navy Stores. Headquarters soon outgrew this accommodation and, in anticipation, Trudie bought a pleasant small house, 26 Eccleston Street, to which Headquarters moved in 1921 as Trudie's tenants. In 1926, when extra space was again needed, a move was made to 39 Eccleston Street where Headquarters has since remained.

The National Federation was also exceptionally fortunate in its senior salaried staff, whom Trudie helped to pick with great good judgement. Early in 1920, Mrs Inez Jenkins (then Miss Ferguson) was chosen as General Secretary. She was very young for the job and looked even younger, but Trudie always maintained that if a person was no good at 26, he or she never would be any good. Ten years later she was succeeded by the Hon. (now Dame) Frances Farrer. The admiration and affection that both acquired for Trudie in their close working association was fully returned, and she had the greatest respect for their ability and devotion to the Movement. The chief of the organizing staff was Mrs Nugent Harris, who was also Editor of *Home and Country*, the Institutes' journal. As well as greatly admiring her enthusiasm and efficiency, Trudie paid tribute to her 'standards of humour and kindliness, which were a lesson to all of us.' Under Mrs Nugent Harris was a small band of regular organizers, as well as the numerous voluntary County organizers in every county for whose training she was responsible.

(vii)

What were the personal qualities that Trudie herself brought to the Federation? In the first place, she possessed to the full a leader's fundamental virtues of courage, truth and absolute fairness and honesty. But what was more unusual—especially perhaps in a

Receiving the C.B.E., 1920

With H.M. Queen Mary
at a Women's Institute
Handicrafts Exhibition,
1938

woman—was her sense of balance and proportion, and her objective outlook which regarded everything in an impersonal, disinterested way. This greatly helped to free the whole movement from personal issues. She had, too, as part of her Pearson inheritance, the gift of a clear concise mind that quickly grasped the essentials of a problem or situation. This she herself regarded as perhaps the most important mental quality. Once, when discussing some problem with her Cambridge educated daughter who had run off at a tangent, she demanded what use there was in a University education if it did not teach you to recognize red herrings? It followed that any form of muddled thinking or pretentiousness was anathema to her. She expected other people to be as direct as she was and to be as little offended by plain speaking. As an older member of the Executive Committee told a new member, 'Lady Denman cannot bear a yes man. If you disagree with her, say so, but mind you know what you are talking about.' And, as Trudie's eventual successor in the Chairmanship, Lady Albemarle, recalls, it was through standing up to Trudie that she first came into her notice. Lady Bury (as Lady Albemarle then was) was Chairman of the Norfolk Federation when she first joined the Executive Committee. A somewhat contentious question had arisen in Norfolk and Trudie had herself placed it on the Executive Committee's agenda. When the item was reached, Trudie asked Lady Bury for her comments. Lady Bury replied that she had no comment to make, as she had not asked for the question to be put on the agenda and that it was up to Lady Denman to comment on it. Trudie was delighted at this rebuff by the Executive's new member. 'You can't put anything across Lady Bury,' she said. Trudie was, in fact, an excellent spotter of talent, especially amongst the young, and the appointments she made were singularly happy.

Writing did not come easily to Trudie, though she took infinite pains to teach herself the art of good clear drafting. She was a superb critic of other people's draftsmanship, with an eagle eye for inaccuracies, illogicality or profuseness. She also had a sure instinct for knowing what ordinary people thought and felt. She would read through a draft put in front of her, then read through it again very slowly and say, 'This would be interpreted by Mrs Smith as meaning so and so, and you don't want that reaction do you?'; or 'Mrs Smith wouldn't know that you meant so and so; you must make it plain to me, an ordinary person. If I can't understand it, Mrs Smith can't.'

What most endeared her to her colleagues and subordinates was her infectious gaiety and sense of fun. On the Executive Committee many a difficult corner would be turned by her light touch and her capacity to make a joke at the right moment. After Trudie's death, Dame Frances Farrer recalled 'the sense of flatness which enveloped us on the rare occasions when Lady Denman was absent from a meeting. How sadly missed were the pungent comments, the sly digs and the unerring sense of humour.' And Dame Frances's predecessor, Mrs Jenkins, tells of her delight in watching her Chairman's eyes getting larger and larger when something amusing was coming, until the moment came and Trudie collapsed in laughter.

Accompanying all these gifts was a very genuine humility, utterly uncorrupted by power. Once, in private conversation, she said to Lady Listowel, a member of the Executive, 'If I *am* a good Chairman, it is because my mind does not work too quickly, not quicker than the average person's.' Her diffidence and her inherent shyness and reserve made some people find her cold and formidable. But in contrast to her general shyness, she was always completely at ease with ordinary Institute members or with land girls. At large meetings or rallies it was with the rank and file, instead of the officers and social 'high ups', that she liked to mingle and talk. Her forthrightness and her inability always to resist baiting the woolly-minded also made her sometimes seem intimidating. Once a somewhat tiresome elderly Institute President buttonholed Trudie at an Annual Meeting and gushingly said, '*I* have been a President longer than *you* have, Lady Denman.' To which Trudie smilingly replied, 'Well, it's quite time *you* retired and *I* did too.' Trudie's shyness and diffidence also prevented her from becoming a good personal teacher, excellent as she was at presiding at Conferences on training. Those workng for her were seldom directly told what she wanted them to do;

they could only learn by watching her in action. Lady Albemarle tells how, when she and Lady Brunner were Trudie's Vice-Chairmen, they tried in vain in office hours to find out what she expected of them. Finally, in despair, they arranged to get her out to lunch with them, thinking that they could then really tackle her. But at lunch she skilfully steered the conversation on to other topics and went away without leaving them any the wiser.

The highly efficient work of the National Federation's Executive Committee formed, of course, the core of the whole Movement's rapid development on sure and sound lines. All who served on the Executive Committee during the thirty years of Trudie's Chairmanship testified to her masterly conduct of its business, to her detached wisdom and judgement that gave all the members an absolute sense of security, to her capacity for keeping discussion clear and to the point and for steering the Committee to reach precise decisions, and to the light-hearted alertness that, after long days of business, left the members fresh and interested and looking forward to the next meeting.

But it was as she presided year by year over their Annual General Meeting that most Institute members knew and still remember their first Chairman. The Annual General Meeting was the great occasion in the Institute year, when delegates from villages in every county in England and Wales came to London in such growing numbers as to compel the Meeting to move in 1923 from the Kingsway Hall to the much larger Queen's Hall and, finally in 1931, to the Albert Hall. (In 1937 the delegates numbered over 5,300, with nearly 2,000 visitors.) The delegates who attended this 'Country Women's Parliament', as it was often called, represented up to ninety per cent of all the Institutes, and their debates and resolutions gave collective expression to rural women's views. No other woman's organization could hold an annual meeting of such a size and representative character, nor one whose influence commanded the presence of Cabinet Ministers and the attention of the National press.

For thirty years Trudie presided over this Parliament with superb skill and mastery. The atmosphere in the huge Hall would tense as the delegates saw their Chairman, easily distinguishable by the fine carriage of her head with its crown of red-gold hair, lead the procession on to the platform. In a few minutes she would have the audience in her hands, alert, attentive, interested and ready to respond to and obey her rulings, given in a voice low-pitched and so clear that it could be heard in the farthest gallery even before the days of loud-speakers. A newspaper report of one of the Annual General Meetings gives this picture of the Chairman.

'She was splendid. She never faltered. She cut short a few of the more verbose and kept others to the point; but she was always ready to help on the more modest, encourage the expression of views, deal swiftly and certainly with a few difficult points of order that arose. She held the whole meeting in her hand, yet never once abused her remarkable influence upon a gathering collected from every corner of England and Wales. By the end of the day she seemed the personal friend of everybody present.'

Most moving was the ovation which each year the delegates gave to Trudie. It seemed as if all the women wanted to convey their personal gratitude for what she had done for them; and it was with this feeling of personal affection and loyalty to their Chairman that the delegates returned to their villages to transmit to their fellow members, in their report of the Parliament in London, their sense of pride in and responsibility for the ever-growing influence of countrywomen united in their Institutes under Lady Denman's leadership.

CHAPTER VIII

The Family Planning Association

The year 1930 saw Trudie embarking on the second major interest of her public life. If her name is less widely associated with the Family Planning Association than it is with the Women's Institutes, the former was a cause to which she devoted herself equally whole-heartedly. It was to retain her allegiance even when ill-health had compelled her to give up all her other public work. As in the case of the Women's Institutes, Trudie was the Family Planning Association's first Chairman and played an equally leading role in the Association's development.

In 1798, the Reverend Thomas Malthus had published his *Essay on Population*, startling his contemporaries with his thesis that, however well ordered society might be, unrestricted reproduction must eventually lead to poverty and misery for the majority of the human race. As a clergyman he could not bring himself to face the idea of contraception. Late marriage was therefore the remedy that he advocated. Radical writers who followed Malthus in the early nineteenth century had not, however, the same inhibitions, and a number of works were published pointing to birth control as the answer to the Malthusian problem. These works included Dr Knowlton's *Fruits of Philosophy*, published in 1833. Twenty years later the scientific basis of neo-Malthusianism, as it was subsequently called, was put forward by Dr George Drysdale in his *Elements of Social Science*. In this, Drysdale argued that the use of contraceptives was the only way to harmonize mankind's two strongest needs, food and sex-gratification. Charles Bradlaugh, the radical publicist and member of Parliament, championed Drysdale's cause and, in 1875, brought the whole issue into the widest public notice when he and Mrs Besant deliberately invited police prosecution by republishing and selling Dr Knowlton's cautiously worded pamphlet of 1833. At their famous trial Bradlaugh and Mrs Besant were found guilty of

'unlawfully and wickedly devising, contriving, and intending, as much as in them lay, to vitiate and corrupt the morals as well of youth as of divers other subjects of the Queen, and to incite and encourage the said subjects to indecent, obscene, unnatural and immoral practices, and bring them to a state of wickedness, lewdness and debauchery.'

They were sentenced to prison, although Bradlaugh succeeded in getting the indictment quashed on appeal. Whatever the verdict of the jury, Bradlaugh's most able and courageous defence at the trial won a notable victory in opening the door to the neo-Malthusian movement and to the more rational treatment of a subject which had hitherto been merely a target for every kind of prejudice and calumny. In his defence, Bradlaugh had arraigned over-population as the cause of misery, poverty, vice, crime and disease. He had shown the futility of Malthus's idea of late marriage or of preaching celibacy as a cure, painting a moving picture of the life of the poor and ignorant agricultural labourer, narrowly bounded by his toil, his comfortless home, the beer-house, the poorhouse and the grave, for whom mere sexual gratification was often the chief pleasure.

In fact, the consequences of ignorance and prejudice did not only affect the lives of the poor and uneducated at that time. Mrs Gladstone, moving in aristocratic Whig circles, was in constant anxiety over the pregnancies of her delicate sister, Lady Lyttleton, who bore seven children in nine years and eventually five more. 'I trust you are safe from any baby,' Mrs Gladstone often wrote to her sister, adding in one letter, 'It really is wrong, people being made ill by having "tant d'enfants".' Lady Lyttleton had her eleventh child in Mrs Gladstone's house so that her sister could nurse her. The doctor pronounced the warning that a twelfth child would mean Lady Lyttleton's certain death. In spite of this, to her sister's grief and dismay, she was again pregnant a few months later. She died in her sister's arms shortly after the birth of her twelfth child. Galsworthy's portrait of Mr Baxter, the Rector, and his wife in *The Country House* gives another and later example of the only too common cruelty inflicted on women by ignorance and masculine selfishness among the well-to-do.

Even after the Bradlaugh-Besant trial, discussion of birth control was mainly confined to intellectual circles such as the neo-Malthusian League, and was carried on more in the academic context of the balance between population trends and economic resources than in terms of the problems of individual men and women. No great change in attitude came about, in fact, until immediately after World War I, when Dr Marie Stopes transformed the thoughts of her generation about the physical aspects of marriage. In her books, *Married Love* and *Wise Parenthood*, she discussed physical love and methods of contraception with uninhibited candour in order that her readers should be able to attain her ideal of marriage as a partnership of equals, expressed in physical relations and in deliberate parenthood free from the fear of unwanted pregnancies. Highly emotional and imbued with quasi-religious fervour, Marie Stopes's writings were not addressed to academic circles but to ordinary, inarticulate men and women. Her books at once achieved an enormous circulation, making birth control a question for discussion by the masses, and a matter of direct, practical concern to innumerable husbands and wives.

Unafraid of notoriety and only encouraged by the opposition of those who disagreed with her on religious grounds, were shocked by her breach of the taboos of good taste, or disliked her unscientific approach, Marie Stopes proceeded to use the money from her books to help establish pioneer clinics in London and one or two other cities through her Society for Constructive Birth Control. Before long four other Birth Control Societies had been formed and clinics were being established in other cities, in spite of much official obstruction and hysterical religious opposition, particularly from Roman Catholics. The *Catholic Herald* described the officers of the Manchester clinic as 'shameless . . . insolent . . . underbred . . . overdressed, overfed and childless . . . who publicly flaunted cigarettes between their painted lips', and whose aim was to 'do something to stop the wretched workers from overrunning the country.' Not to be outdone, the Bishop of Salford complained from the pulpit that the police were powerless 'to put these people away'. He urged fathers and mothers to 'hound them out of the district'. Nevertheless, so much progress was made that in April 1930 a conference was held in London on the 'giving of information on birth control by Public Health Authorities'. The conference passed a resolution calling upon the Ministry of Health to 'recognize the desirability of making available medical information on birth control to married women who need it.' As a next step, some of the leaders in the birth control movement, notably Mrs Eva Hubback and Mrs Hugh Dalton, felt that it was desirable to form a body to centralize the work of the five existing birth control societies. They also felt that the movement needed as its head a woman of recognized position and proved ability to help in obtaining finance and to give it the respectability and standing which it still lacked. As their first choice Mrs Hubback and Mrs Dalton turned to Lady Denman.

It was a cause in which Trudie had already become interested. She had supported the Walworth Women's Welfare Centre founded by Dr and Mrs Drysdale as early as 1921, and had since given money to help Dr Stopes's and other clinics. Her interest did not stem from any academic occupation with world economic trends. Like Bradlaugh and Marie Stopes, her concern was with the lives of individuals. In Australia and at home she had seen for herself the results of unchecked child-bearing, particularly among countrywomen; and all her passionate sense of justice had been roused by the unfairness that it was on the wife that the penalty for married ignorance and selfishness mainly fell. Trudie had the sympathy and the imagination to see what this meant in terms of the lives of poor women, living in constant terror of another pregnancy when they were already prematurely worn out by child-bearing and by the never ceasing struggle to keep health and decency for their families as they outgrew the means and room for their proper support. Whether the home was rich or poor, Trudie felt strongly that the wife had a right to a share in the control of her own and her family's destiny. The well-to-do she knew, could and did obtain advice of some sort from their own doctors. It was, she felt, a grave injustice to withhold such advice and help from the poor.

On Trudie's agreeing to accept this new responsibility, a meeting was held in the drawing-room of 43 Upper Grosvenor Street, which had become her London home when she left Buckingham Gate in 1921. At this meeting, Mr Ernest Thurtle, the Labour member of Parliament, and Dr Marie Stopes proposed a resolution that the National Birth Control Council should be brought into being, and Trudie was elected the new Council's Chairman.

It would have been understandable if, with all her other commitments, Trudie had felt that financial help and passive encouragement were the most she could offer. But her strong sense of duty and her desire to aid a cause in which she so deeply believed compelled her to throw her whole vital energy and all her experience into the active leadership of the new movement. She knew that it would prove no light assignment—she was later to say that it was the most difficult job she had ever undertaken—and that it would require courage and fortitude to meet the prejudice which still surrounded the whole subject and to which she would now be publicly exposed. At the 1918 Lambeth Conference, the Bishops of the Anglican Church had condemned all birth control practices outright. At the recent 1930 Lambeth Conference they had, however, gone so far as to commit themselves to the cautious statement that, 'where there is such a clearly felt moral obligation to limit or avoid parenthood, and where there is a morally sound reason for avoiding complete abstinence, the Conference agrees that other methods may be used'. But the Roman Catholic hierarchy remained adamant in opposition, and Trudie knew that devout churchwomen of all denominations in the Women's Institute movement would be shocked and pained at the head of their movement thus publicly associating herself with something that was hardly respectable, even if, in all cases, it was not expressly forbidden.

Trudie's first steps were to let the new Council have the use of two rooms in the house at 26 Eccleston Street which she owned, and to help in the appointment of a General Secretary. It so happened that she had just been called upon to assist in making an important appointment to the Institutes' headquarters staff. The final choice had been between two candidates, and Trudie had left this to Miss Farrer who had selected the one with Institute organizing experience. Trudie had been much impressed by the other, Mrs Margaret Pyke, whom the Council now appointed as their General Secretary. It was not only to prove an outstanding appointment for the future of the Council, but in Margaret Pyke Trudie was to find one of her closest and most devoted friends for the rest of her life.

Almost simultaneously with the starting of the new Council, the Ministry of Health issued its memorandum 153. Addressed to Local Authorities, this document broke entirely new official ground by permitting them to establish birth control clinics and to give contraceptive advice in their maternity centres. Only expectant and nursing mothers could, however, be allowed to make use of such services, and then with the strict proviso that advice could only be given in cases where further pregnancy would be detrimental to health. So great was official caution in approaching this contentious subject that the purpose of the document, with its whole emphasis on the negative, might well have appeared to be more designed as a warning to local authorities than as an encouragement to positive action. Nevertheless, the document gave the Council an immediate objective in bringing pressure to bear on the Local Authorities through the crack in the door that the Ministry had thus opened. The Council, therefore, quickly produced its first leaflet entitled *Birth Control and Public Health Authorities*. This was sent out to all authorities, to the annoyance of the Ministry who considered it unnecessary as well as impertinent for the Council to try to reinforce the cautious and negative verbiage of the official memorandum by interpreting it in simple, positive terms. The Council also started a direct attack on the local authorities in the distressed areas where the need for advice on birth control seemed to be greatest, Trudie sending Mrs Pyke up to Tyneside to visit Medical Officers and anyone else she could interest and to arrange for the appointment of a part-time local organizer to follow up her work. That year (1930) saw the Council's first Annual General Meeting, held at the Central Hall, Westminster, with Trudie presiding.

In face of the Council's pressure, the Ministry next year felt obliged to issue a second memorandum emphasizing that Local Authorities had no power to establish Birth Control Clinics as such, and again defining the strict limits under which contraceptive advice might be given. It was clear that official caution was too great to give the Council much chance of success if it relied solely on bringing pressure on Local Authorities. Trudie and her Executive Committee therefore resolved to alter the direction of their attack and to concentrate their efforts on helping to form voluntary clinics wherever the Local Authority refused or was unable to take action. The Council also altered its title to that of the 'National Birth Control Association', and acquired, through Trudie's personal efforts, a President in the person of the eminent physician Sir Thomas (later Lord) Horder. Professor (later Sir) Julian Huxley and Lady Limerick were Vice-Presidents, and distinguished original members of the Association Executive were Mrs Mary Stocks and Dr Blacker, the Secretary of the Eugenics Society. A little later Lady Maureen Stanley was co-opted while, in 1935, the Executive was further reinforced on its medical side by Sir Walter Langdon Brown who wrote a pamphlet, *The Ethics of Birth Control*, which was of much value to the Association.

The next year (1932) was an eventful one. In the spring, an agreement was reached in Plymouth whereby the Local Authority loaned premises for a voluntary clinic. The Ministry raised no objection to such co-operation which was to form a very useful pattern for future work. There was also a victory in Ealing, where the Local Authority, having decided to start a municipal clinic, encountered violent opposition. Rival meetings were held and the local paper was filled with letters for and against the clinic, but Ealing stuck to its guns. Following a further tour by Mrs Pyke, an organizer was appointed for South Wales, and the Association held its first medical conference, attended by 200 doctors and laboratory workers, while the Maternity and Child Welfare section of the Royal Sanitary Institute devoted a whole session of its conference to the subject of birth control.

Things were certainly moving forward when, in 1933, the British Medical Association lent its premises to the National Birth Control Association for a conference attended by 125 Medical Officers of Health and private practitioners, and when representatives of the Association addressed a meeting of Members of Parliament at the House of Commons. In 1935, after five years' work, sixty-six municipal clinics had been formed and forty-seven voluntary clinics. By 1939 the Association had formed sixty-seven branches, of which sixty-three ran clinics, many of them aided or lent premises by Local Authorities, eighty-four of whom were now directly giving birth control advice. In 1938 the Association moved into larger premises, lent rent-free by the Eugenics Society. The next year the Association again changed its name and became the Family Planning Association. From the start, Trudie had been insistent that birth control was not merely designed to prevent unwanted pregnancies, but had the positive object of the proper spacing of families so that every child should have a chance of health and happiness. The Association's change of title served better to express its actual work which, as well as promoting facilities for contraception, now included the giving of advice on infertility and gynaecological and other marital difficulties.

Throughout these formative years, Trudie was not only nursing the Association financially; she was also devoting to its growth the same control and leadership that had inspired the Women's Institutes movement. At the Executive Committee meetings, she displayed the same clarity of thought and direction, and the same ruthlessness in checking repetitive or aimless discussion. 'Haven't we been clever,' she would say, 'we are half an hour before time. Now we can go and play or do something useful.' As she once wrote to one of her nieces, she believed that the art of chairmanship was 'to get the views of the silent ones and to stop the others discussing items which are not on the agenda.' Above all, she brought to the Family Planning Association the gay and humorous approach and turn of phrase that carried the committee through its difficult discussions. 'Well, we *are* learning,' she would remark when something particularly startling had been disclosed; or, when she wished to curtail the pompous and the prolix, she would jokingly observe, 'How very interesting, I haven't heard that since nineteen hundred and two!'

Scrupulous as she always was to hear every side of a question, she never interpreted chairmanship as neutrality, but believed that a chairman must exercise leadership. Nowhere did she have more need to deploy all her resources than on the Family Planning Executive, where Dr Marie Stopes had, from the first, proved to be a very difficult member. All the defects of her qualities conspired to prevent her from co-operating on equal terms with other people; and her dogmatic and emotional approach to any subject was the opposite of Trudie's own objective and practical standpoint. But, from admiration for Dr Stopes's courage and splendid achievements, Trudie went out of her way to handle her with the greatest tact, according her a latitude which, as a chairman, she never extended to others. It was not, however, without relief that, in 1933, Trudie accepted her resignation and that of her Society of Constructive Birth Control from the Association. Her resignation certainly eased Trudie's task of securing governmental, medical and public acceptance for the Association's aims.

Besides always presiding at the Executive Committee's monthly meetings, and travelling to take the chair at conferences of branches, Trudie entered the public arena in support of the Association's work on numerous occasions. Family Planning had not only still to face the bitter prejudice of many Church leaders (Mrs Bramwell Booth of the Salvation Army, for instance, in an article in the *Daily Mirror* described birth control as 'utterly wrong and not in God's plan' and alleged 'that young girls were being destroyed in great numbers every year because of it', while the President of the Catholic Women's League prophesied 'race suicide and moral degeneracy'); there was also patriotic opposition on national and imperial grounds.

Strange as it now seems to us, only twenty years later, leading demographic experts were then predicting with the utmost, if singularly misplaced, confidence that a declining birth-rate would bring the population of the United Kingdom to below thirty million by the end of the century. The danger to Britain and to the white Dominions, proclaimed the experts, lay not in over-population but in depopulation, and they painted a picture of birth control bringing about the decay and final extinction of the British Empire. In her speeches and written replies to such charges, Trudie countered by emphasizing that the Association's aim was not the prevention of births but the planning of the family. It was her firm conviction—in which she was to be proved right—that once women had knowledge of and confidence in birth control, there would be fewer childless couples and only children. She also pointed out that contraceptive methods might be the means but were not the cause of a declining birth-rate, whose remedy lay in the improvement of economic and social conditions, and that the withholding of information on scientific contraception led to an increase in abortions and in maternal mortality. Her final argu-ment was that she believed 'birth control to be practised by scientific or unscientific methods. All who are rich enough can get advice from a doctor. It is not fair to try to prevent the poor people who are far more overcrowded and have far more difficulties to contend with from getting the information on the subject which is available to the rich.'

In a letter to a friend, written in 1933, Trudie characteristically described how difficult she found her family planning work.

'There have been moments,' she wrote, 'when I have thought that Mrs Jenkins, Miss Hadow and I must be distinctly bright, because our Women's Institutes have gone so well. Fortunately, I have generally realized that the Institutes just flourish by themselves and that even in counties where the leaders are incredibly stupid, they still survive. But the National Birth Control Association is knocking out all my remaining conceit.'

Her letter went on to tell of how she seemed unable even to get the simplest ideas into the minds of some of her distinguished male colleagues:

'Having helped to tackle Carnegie Trustees, Development Commissioners, County Council Associations and every kind of Government Department and never having come empty away, this complete lack of success was one of the surprises of my young life! I can hardly believe it has really happened. . . . I am now on my way back from Sheffield where with great difficulty an audience of 19 women and 1 man was collected to hear me (N.B. my usual meetings in the country [for the Institutes] vary between two and seven hundred) so I now understand and grasp the fundamental fact that I have up to now had very easy jobs and that in this one which does want some intelligence, I certainly don't shine! However I think I have spiked Dr . . . .'s guns, and the minute meeting in Sheffield from which I have just come was I think quite useful. They were dour to start with, but I think I persuaded the Chairman of the Health Committee (a nice old woman) that she is one of the pioneers of this great National Birth Control Association movement! This was possible because, although she has always been against birth control, a fortnight ago they started stocking contraceptive appliances in the Welfare Centre and giving advice when they think it necessary. I was told that this was done to make it more difficult to start a voluntary clinic, but I think that if the Sheffield people work up a great demand for information amongst the women attending the clinic and then keep on congratulating the old girl on the great work she has done, she may really come to believe that she is one of our supporters. From all this you will see that I have bobbed up again and that the humble phase is safely over!'

The Association was always short of funds and could not have kept going without the direct financial help given by Trudie and the Pearson family, and without the special money-raising efforts which she sponsored with the aid of her friend Sir Mark Grant-Sturgis whom she persuaded to become Chairman of the Association's Finance Sub-Committee. These included a dinner at Claridge's which raised £1,350, a regional bridge tournament, and a Gala Ballet at the Cambridge Theatre in London with special assistance from Sir Malcolm Sargent, Ninette de Valois and Marie Rambert. But Trudie's most valuable contribution was perhaps the way in which she made the fullest use of her reputation and influence to gain respectability and prestige for a movement which, initially, had enjoyed so little of either. She never hesitated to tackle Cabinet Ministers and Government Departments—she was one of the speakers on a deputation to the Ministry of Health in 1937, and at the end of that year, she gave evidence before the Interdepartmental Committee on Abortion —while the hospitable resources of her home at 43 Upper Grosvenor Street were in constant employment for luncheons, dinners and receptions to guests from the 'Establishment' who she thought might assist the cause.

Such were the foundations laid by Trudie in the years before the war. It is due to these pioneer efforts that the Family Planning Association now enjoys a position and an influence that would have been unthinkable even in 1939. In the post-war developments Trudie, until her death, was to continue to play her full part.

CHAPTER IX

More Public Activities

(i)

The Women's Institutes and the Family Planning Association, time and energy absorbing as they were, did not by any means exhaust the public activities which Trudie undertook in the years between the wars. One was only short-lived. In 1920, she was among the first batch of women to be invited by the Lord Chancellor to become Justices of the Peace, as the result of the Sex Disability (Removal) Bill passed by Parliament in 1919. In its preamble the Bill stated, 'a person shall not be disqualified by sex or marriage from the exercise of any public function, or from being appointed to or holding any civil or judicial office or post, or from assuming or carrying on any civil profession or vocation, or from admission to any incorporated society.' All public offices held under the Crown were thus opened up to women, so that today there are women mayors and aldermen, Queen's Counsel, prison Governors and permanent heads of Departments of State.

Trudie duly took her place on the bench at Hayward's Heath. It was not long, however, before she resigned. She thought that the Chairman was weak and allowed the Clerk to bully witnesses outrageously. Since the Chairman was unlikely to resign and the Clerk could not be removed, she felt that she had better things to do than to sit in Court fretted and frustrated by matters which she had no power to alter.

Another activity, of which as a very keen if only moderately-skilled golfer she was immensely proud, was her Presidency of the Ladies' Golf Union. She was elected President and Chairman in 1933, in succession to Lady Rhondda, and held this position until her resignation in 1938. She always took the greatest trouble over her clothes and her speech at the Union's annual dinner, when her humour and lightness of touch exactly suited the occasion. The

Union's Executive Council had need of all her experience and skill, since a most difficult problem arose over the amateur status of members who took payment for writing articles or books on golf. Starting at the end of 1933, Trudie had to conduct long negotiations with the Royal and Ancient Golf Club of St Andrews. The R and A gave their opinion that such members were not eligible to continue to play as amateurs, but when the L.G.U. returned one member's entrance fee for a match, they were threatened with a writ. Trudie was compelled, on behalf of the L.G.U., to seek the advice of Counsel, who wrote to her that the statement she proposed to make 'could not be bettered . . . it is strictly accurate, just and sympathetic.' Although, on Trudie's advice, the Executive Council set up an Amateur Status Committee to help players who needed advice, the trouble continued to crop up and had not been finally resolved at the time of Trudie's resignation. All this caused much work and worry to the President, but Trudie's clear and quick perception and her good humour were of the greatest value to the L.G.U. in these difficult years. It was also characteristic of Trudie that one of her early acts as President was to arrange for the institution of a pension fund for the staff.

Then there was her work for the Land Settlement Association and for the Carnegie United Kingdom Trust. Prolonged and general urban unemployment was the greatest social evil of the nineteen thirties. As one means of alleviation, the Society of Friends started a small experimental scheme for the provision of allotments and smallholdings in the hope that, through working on these, victims of unemployment might earn a living wage and win back their self-respect. Lionel Hichens, the Chairman of Cammell-Laird's, the shipbuilders, and a Director of many other industrial enterprises, became interested in the scheme and brought it to the attention of the Carnegie United Kingdom Trust of which he was a member. This trust had been founded in 1913 when the Scottish-American millionaire, Andrew Carnegie, who had for many years given large sums of money to British Local Authorities for public libraries and to the Churches for the provision of organs, executed a deed setting up the Trust with a capital sum of $10,000,000, the income from which was to be used 'for the improvement of the well-being of the masses of the people in Great Britain and Ireland.' Since 1913, nearly half of the income had gone to libraries, but very substantial sums had also been allotted to such causes as physical welfare and playing fields, music and drama activities and rural development and social service.

Discussions by the Trustees came to the conclusion that settlers on smallholdings should be established as independent units with a co-operative system of buying and selling, and not merely as wage earners; and that a central body should be set up to supervise any settlements and to administer any funds provided by the State and by voluntary contributions. After calling a conference early in 1934 which approved these ideas, the Trustees decided to adopt land settlement as a major part of their policy for their next quinquennium, beginning in 1936. In May 1934 the Minister of Agriculture, Mr Walter Elliot, announced that the Government favoured the setting up of a Central Land Settlement Association and would contribute £1 for every £2 raised by the Association from voluntary sources. As a result, the Land Settlement Association was formed in July, with Sir Percy Jackson, the Vice-Chairman of the Carnegie Trust, as its first Chairman. The Association soon found itself not only looking after its own settlement schemes financed from voluntary plus Government sources, but also the settlement schemes financed wholly by the Government under their new Act for helping the special areas where unemployment was worst, the special areas Commissioner being Mr (later Sir) Malcolm Stewart, who had been closely associated with the Society of Friends and had, from his own purse, bought the first settlement estate at Potton in Bedfordshire. As Special Areas Commissioner, Mr Stewart at once appointed the Land Settlement Association as his agent for his resettlement schemes, while the Government's offer to the Association in respect of voluntary-financed schemes was increased to a £1 for £1 basis. The Carnegie Trust had already given £10,000 for the development of the Potton estate and before long allotted a further £150,000 for settlement schemes in England and Wales under the aegis of the Land Settlement Association with its central marketing organization.

Trudie had herself brought a family from the distressed areas to Balcombe and had housed and employed them on the estate. She had also been one of the first to contribute money for land settlement and was early elected to the Executive Committee of the Association. It was the first attempt that had been made anywhere in the world to settle unemployed urban industrial workers on the land as independent, self-supporting smallholders, and she gave unwavering support in time and money to make the experiment a success. Others saw the difficulty of changing the mentality of a wage-earner to that of an independent capitalist, but Trudie's imaginative yet practical mind also realized the problem that would be created for the settler's wife, flung into an unfamiliar social environment and faced with new domestic worries in looking after her family under conditions wholly different from those she had known in an overcrowded tenement. At Trudie's instigation, therefore, the Association agreed in 1938 to set up a Recreation Welfare Sub-Committee with Trudie as its Chairman. Her first step was to send out a circular letter to all those concerned with the Land Settlement estates, inviting them to send representatives to a week-end conference at her own home at Balcombe.

'There are many problems to be solved,' she wrote in her letter, 'before the industrial worker and his wife can become contented small-holders. Technical training on agriculture is given to the men, but help and advice on the human and educational needs of a new and strange community are very much wanted and cannot always be given by the Wardens of the Estates whose hands are already full . . . We want to appoint two or three representatives of the Land Settlement Association in each locality in which Estates have been formed. These representatives would, we hope, form the nucleus of a Welfare and Recreation Committee. My personal view is that these representatives would probably have two main functions.

'1. Committee side: To advise how best settlers can take advantage of the facilities offered by the County Councils and by local voluntary bodies, for example, formation of maternal and child welfare clinics, dental treatment, classes on cooking and dressmaking etc.

'2. The Personal side: To visit the settlers' wives and help them to face their many strange problems. To point out to them, for instance, that it is more healthy and economic to use garden produce rather than tinned vegetables, but that, at the same time, it is not economic to live chiefly on home produced eggs at a time when they are fetching high prices in the market. . . .

I believe if it can be shown that co-operative small holdings can be made a success, it will help towards the solution of two of the main problems with which this country is faced—the decrease in the production of home grown food and the migration from the country to the towns.'

The four-day Balcombe conference took place at the end of October (1938) when fifteen delegates as well as a number of invited lecturers crowded the house as Trudie's guests. She took the chair throughout and herself gave a talk on the help that could be afforded by the Women's Institutes, pointing out that the Institutes were a means of bringing the settlers' wives into friendly contact with countrywomen, and showing how the Institutes could help on the social side and with educational work. She also stressed how, through the Institutes, pressure could be brought on the local authorities to provide the essential services. 'The County Federations,' she said, 'represent a very large body of public opinion, and representations made by them to the local authorities invariably receive due consideration.'

With the Carnegie Trust finding the cost of the first experiments, Trudie's sub-committee began operations, she herself devoting much time to its detailed work. Full-time welfare officers were appointed in addition to part-time workers and local committees, and Trudie interviewed them all. Huts or other buildings were provided and equipped to act as community centres on the estates; wives and children in industrial areas were prepared for the move; loans were made for buying proper country clothing; links were established with the local health services; educational talks were arranged for the women; activities organized for young people, and playing fields provided. But the outbreak of war a year later produced a complete change in the situation. The Land Settlement Association's purpose had to be altered, almost overnight, from settling unemployed on the land to utilizing the existing estates to their utmost capacity for the production of food. When war was declared, Trudie was forced, because of her Land Army responsibilities, to delegate her work to the Vice-Chairman of the Association. She soon found herself in disagreement with the Executive Committee when they dismissed the Director of the Association and then refused him a hearing. Feeling that she could not share the responsibility for work with which she was not in close touch, she resigned from the Committee.

In the meantime, however, Trudie's active interest in Land Settlement had brought her to the notice of the Carnegie United Kingdom Trustees, and, in March 1938, they had invited her to become a Life Trustee in place of the late Miss Elizabeth Haldane. She was at once appointed to the Trust's Executive Committee and to its Policy and Music sub-committees. This was no light assignment for one already so hard-worked, involving, as it sometimes did, journeys to Scotland for the meetings of the Trust.

But Trudie found much that was of special interest to her in the Trust's activities beside land settlement, which, as we have seen, had become one of the Trust's major beneficiaries. The help given for the building and improvement of Village Halls, the grants to Rural Community Councils, and the assistance to Music and Drama in rural areas were all matters of direct concern to Trudie as head of the Women's Institutes, apart from such direct grants to the Institutes as those for the produce marketing scheme and for the making of instructional films on countrywomen's handicrafts. Other projects which the Trust was helping to finance, in which Trudie was particularly concerned, were the Nutrition Inquiry and the Population Investigation Committee which was examining the housing requirements of families and the reasons which deterred young married couples from having children. And, in their discussions on all these projects, her fellow

Trustees profited greatly, in the words of one of them, by her 'wide experience and grasp of affairs, her wisdom and unfailing sympathy with all social amelioration of every kind, which made her an ideal Trustee.'

Studley College was yet another activity in which she became involved through her concern with women's part in rural life. The College had been founded in 1898 in order to train young women in dairy farming and in horticulture. In the nineteen-thirties, when a development scheme was launched to buy the College buildings, Trudie became a Governor and Chairman of the Appeals Committee, which held most of its meetings at her London house. Not content with giving generous financial help, she also spent much time and energy in support of the College's successful development.

(ii)

At the end of 1933 Trudie entered a wholly new field of activity when she became a Director of the Westminster Press. The Pearson family connection with newspapers dated from as far back as 1908, when her father had joined the syndicate which owned the Liberal London evening paper, the *Westminster Gazette*, whose editor was the distinguished Liberal political writer, J. A. Spender. Then, shortly after the end of the First World War, Lord Cowdray had acquired the largest interest in an important group of Provincial newspapers, with Sir Charles Starmer as Managing Director. In 1923 a morning edition of the *Westminster Gazette* had taken the place of the London evening paper. Four years later, on the death of Trudie's father, his eldest son Harold, the second Lord Cowdray, inherited the family newspaper responsibilities. The next year (1928) the *Westminster Gazette* was amalgamated with the *Daily News*, another Liberal morning paper, under the name of the *News and Westminster*. As part of the arrangements, Spender, for whose character, ability and judgement all the Pearson family had the highest admiration, was to write for the new paper and to be on its Board and Policy Committee. This did not make for easy relations with the editor, Tom Clarke.

In 1930, a further amalgamation took place with the *Daily Chronicle*, Lloyd George's organ, the new paper being called the *News Chronicle*. Sir Walter Layton was appointed its Chairman and Managing Director, with Tom Clarke its editor. Trouble began to arise almost at once, Spender complaining to Lord Cowdray that he was being crowded out and that, through Lloyd George's influence, the new paper was supporting the Labour rather than the Liberal Party. The Pearson family were no friends of Lloyd George and had not forgotten or forgiven his and Northcliffe's shabby treatment of the first Lord Cowdray over the Air Board in the war. In October 1933 Tom Clarke, the *News Chronicle*'s editor, resigned. It was at this moment that the second Lord Cowdray died, having been pre-deceased earlier in the year by Sir Charles Starmer, the Managing Director of the Westminster Press.

Trudie's younger brother, Clive, was now head of the family newspaper interests, and Trudie and her sister-in-law Beryl, Harold's widow, joined the Board of the Westminster Press. It was not in Trudie's character lightly to assume any responsibility, and she began at once to play an active part on the Board, both as an initiator and as her brother's close consultant. Nor was the responsibility a light one. Apart from the quite distinct affairs of the *News Chronicle*, the Westminster Press Provincial Newspapers Ltd. (to give the Company its full title) at that time owned or controlled sixteen newspaper companies, four general printing businesses and a newspaper feature agency. Its various newspaper companies published four morning papers, nine evening papers, over thirty weekly and sports papers and one Sunday newspaper. The papers in the group ranged from Northumberland in the north to Wiltshire in the west. Their aggregate weekly sale was some six million copies, and the staffs numbered some 3,500.

The editorial policy of the whole group of papers was, of course, the responsibility of the proprietors of the Westminster Press. The aim of the founders of the group had been to give support to the Liberal cause, and the Pearsons had continued this tradition. With the advent of Trudie and her sister-in-law to the Board, an Editorial Policy Committee was set up of which Trudie was an influential member. The Committee met monthly with its political advisers and leader writers to discuss the topics on which it seemed likely that decisions would have to be taken within the next few weeks. Later, the Chairman also gave a monthly dinner party to which was invited a guest speaker whose views would be particularly valuable. Trudie suggested or introduced many of these guests and was herself a regular attendant at the dinners.

The newspapers in the group varied greatly in character and presentation. Trudie strongly supported the policy of encouraging each paper to develop its own individuality and to become an integral part of the community it served. The better to keep in touch with all the papers in the group, she arranged for copies of a number of them to be sent to her each week, so that in the course of a month she saw them all. Her special attention was given to the weeklies circulating in the country districts. She believed that these had an important role to play as a public service for country people, not least in helping to keep local authorities up to the mark. Many were the suggestions that she made for the better presentation of Women's Institute activities and for the handling of news of interest to countrywomen; and, while she realized that local events such as weddings and funerals were of much more importance to those who knew the people concerned than were world events, she was always pleading for wider horizons in the leading and feature articles, and was instrumental in the setting up of an information department as a service for the leader-writers in country weeklies who otherwise had not the opportunity of fully acquainting themselves with many of the specialist questions affecting their readers. Never unreasonable in promoting her own views and particular interests, she was always willing to give the technicians and experts a free hand, provided that the papers consistently supported the broad liberal outlook on which her own sympathies were based.

As was the case with any organization with which she was connected, Trudie made the welfare of the staffs her special concern. Finding that the group's pension fund made no provision for the women employees, and that it would cost an extra £1,000 a year to right what she felt was an injustice, Trudie, backed by her sister-in-law, proposed that a corresponding economy should be made in management costs by reducing the Directors' fees. She and her sister-in-law offered to halve their fees, and, when the other non-salaried Directors agreed to follow suit, the money was available for including the women workers in the pension scheme.

It was also characteristic of Trudie that all her fighting instincts should have been aroused in the winter of 1936–1937 by the forced dismissal of the women workers in the printing department of the two Shields newspapers, when the typographers threatened to strike because the women were not union members. Trudie's inquiries from the Women's Employment Federation showed that while the avowed policy of the printing trade unions was to admit women, this was combined with a refusal to allow women to serve the apprenticeship which would qualify them for union membership. She then took the question up with Labour women members of Parliament and with the General Secretary of the Trades Union Congress, but her efforts led nowhere. All that she could do to mitigate the injustice was to see that proper notice and extra wages were given to all the workers dismissed, with pensions in the cases of old employees or of special hardship. It was also in the tradition of her father's regard for all who worked for him that Trudie should always have gone out of her way to give generous praise for any achievement on the part of the managements of the various companies, and to extend sympathy and understanding over difficulties.

At the start of Trudie's interest in newspapers, however, it was the affairs of the *News Chronicle* rather than those of the Westminster Press newspapers that most occupied her attention. She had hardly taken up her new duties before Spender was writing to her that things had not changed for the better under the new editor and that his articles were being relegated to the wastepaper basket. Trudie and her sister-in-law at once sought the advice of the Liberal Party leaders, Sir Herbert (later Lord) Samuel and Mr Harcourt Johnstone. In the report which she wrote to her brother, Trudie told him that after a frank discussion on the way in which the *News Chronicle* was being given a Labour slant, Samuel had suggested that Lord Lothian might be invited to fill a vacant seat on one of the Management Boards which exercised an influence on the paper's policy. But Lord Lothian refused the invitation on the grounds that the *News Chronicle*, 'while its general political policy may be called Liberal, regards the Labour Party as the natural nucleus of opposition to the Government.'

All through 1934 there were letters, memoranda and meetings between Trudie, her brother and Sir Walter Layton, the paper's Chairman, but Trudie and her brother failed to get Layton and the editorial staff to agree that support at by-elections should be given to the Liberal rather than to the Labour candidate, or that free enterprise should take a more important place in the paper's economic policy. They were able, however, to secure that Spender's articles should again appear so as to give the paper additional Liberal ballast.

In respect of the Westminster Press Provincial Newspapers, much trouble arose over editorial policy at the time of the Munich crisis. The editor-in-chief of the Group and most of the local editors wanted to take the Liberal Party line of opposition to Chamberlain. But Spender had nailed his flag to Chamberlain's mast, and carried Trudie and her brother with him. He wrote to Trudie that the editors were cutting or suppressing his articles, and that they 'seem to treat Chamberlain as a common criminal whom I am trying to shield.' Trudie and her brother agreed that they must give the Prime Minister their support over foreign policy, 'even if it means no longer calling ourselves Liberals', and she wrote to her brother, 'I think Beryl (her sister-in-law) and I can keep the editorial staff on fairly moderate lines at the moment.'

That winter (1938–1939) Spender was in the South of France for his health, but his influence on Trudie's political thinking was as strong as ever.

'Even if you are not in England,' she wrote to him in January, 'you are a tower of strength. Personally I feel it would be almost impossible to fight the policy of our Liberal friends on the papers without you. When arguing with them now, the knowledge that my own feeling of certainty that we must support Chamberlain is backed by your great knowledge, experience and judgement prevents me from being shaken by their flow of words.'

Early in 1939, Trudie refused to renew her £1,250 annual subscription to the Liberal Party. Her decision brought a sad letter from Lady Gladstone, the President of the Women's Liberal Federation, recalling the old days and 'all the help and strength that both your parents gave so generously to the party.' 'I feel I cannot let you go without a struggle,' she added. But Trudie's belief in seventy-six-year-old Spender's judgement remained unshaken.

'It is a chilly business having to damp down the ardours of the idealists,' he wrote to her, 'but their view that we are responsible for everything that goes wrong in the world and ought to intervene to put it right, places a burden on us to which our power is quite unequal. It was one thing for all the powers jointly to undertake to police the world through the League of Nations as it was intended to be; quite another for us or the French to undertake this work against the opposition of the other powers.'

It was not only Trudie who then accepted Spender's views. They were shared by the majority of her countrymen.

In 1937 a further responsibility fell, by family inheritance, on Trudie's broad shoulders. This was the Chairmanship of the Cowdray Club for Nurses. It was an inheritance from her mother. Lady Cowdray's greatest public interest had always been the betterment of the status and conditions of the nursing profession, and when, early in the 1914–1918 war, a College of Nursing had been set up under Royal Charter, she had become the Honorary Treasurer for the appeal for the endowment of the College, and she and her family, including Trudie, had been generous donors. Annie Cowdray had then decided that she and her husband should add to their generosity by the gift of a social club for nurses and professional women. For this purpose she bought the Asquiths' old house in Cavendish Square. She also presented to the College a neighbouring site in Henrietta Street for its own building. In June 1922 she opened the Club as its first Chairman. On the same day she laid the foundation stone for the College building on the adjacent site. Not content with having given the site, the Cowdrays financed the building and equipment of the College which was opened by Queen Mary in 1926. Four years later, when two more adjacent sites had become vacant, Lady Cowdray undertook to pay for building extensions to College and Club provided the College bought the sites. The College and Club thus came to occupy a whole corner site (embracing the sites of four former houses) with a uniform façade in Cavendish Square and an entirely new block in Henrietta Street. All in all, the cost to the Cowdrays was well over £250,000; and Lady Cowdray spent much time in personally choosing the furniture and fittings for the Club and the College, often augmenting her purchases with pieces of furniture from her own homes. Lady Cowdray died in 1932, before all the new building was finished. Her estate was very severely hit by death duties, but her family generously financed the completion of the work.

It was always Lady Cowdray's intention that the activities of the College and the Club should be complementary, and, in fact, the top three floors of the College which she had built were devoted to bedrooms for the Club. For reasons of taxation, the College was made the 'landlord' of the Club, giving it a lease at a nominal rent terminating in 1950. Half the members of the Club's Governing Council were to be members of the College, which was to appoint the Club's Chairman. Fifty-five per cent of the members of the Club were to be nurses and were to pay only half the subscription charged to other professional women. The Club, under Annie Cowdray's personal direction, was soon on its feet, and from 1926 to her death in 1932 it made profits. Unfortunately, these could not be put to reserve, as it was a condition of the lease that nine-tenths of any profits were to go to the College and the remaining tenth to the staff superannuation fund. Lady Cowdray had never envisaged the possibility of any enterprise of hers making losses, but from 1932 the Club began losing money on an increasing scale. This question of losses and the obvious possibilities of clashes of personalities and friction between Club and College were the legacy which Lady Cowdray left to her descendants, notably to her granddaughter, Nancy (later Mrs John Hare), whom Lady Cowdray had put to work in the Club when she left school, starting in the kitchens. Later Mrs Hare served on the Council, but the demands of marriage and children did not leave her much time for Club affairs, which were usually difficult especially in regard to staffing. In 1937, therefore, Mrs Hare asked Trudie, her aunt, for her support. Reluctant as Trudie was to add to her heavy commitments, she felt that the Club was a family responsibility which she could not shirk and that she must reinforce her niece on the Club's Council. As she wrote to her, 'I know something of matrons, and it takes *two* ordinary people to down *one* matron.' Trudie was accordingly appointed by the College as Chairman of the Club. Her first step was to call in accountancy and catering experts to report on how the continuance of the Club's working losses could be avoided. In December (1937) she had the satisfaction of being able to write to the members of the Council that the experts believed that the Club could become self-supporting with some increases in subscriptions and in the dining-room charges.

Difficulties had, however, been brewing between the College and the Club. The former was also in need of money, and although its expanding work required extra accommodation, finance compelled it to lease the new building in which the Club had hoped to obtain extra bedrooms. The College, moreover, began to cast eyes on the three floors of bedrooms in its original building which the Club occupied at a nominal rent.

These looming troubles were not, however, to come to a head and add grievously to Trudie's burdens until the war and after.

Another family responsibility came to Trudie in 1927 when, on her father's death, she joined the Board of S. Pearson and Son, the main holding Company for the varied family interests, and also became a Director of the Cowdray Trust. Here her chief concern was to help her brother Clive carry the burden which fell so largely on his shoulders.

Official recognition of the value of Trudie's public work was not lacking in these years. In 1920 she was made a Companion of the Order of the British Empire in recognition of her war services. Thirteen years later, her work for the Women's Institutes led to her being created Dame Commander of the Order. Forty-nine was a young age for such a high honour. In a letter she described how she went to Buckingham Palace for the investiture

'expecting a few people in ordinary clothes and found about 100 men in lovely uniforms and Miss Horniman and me. Later, Lady . . . . arrived, she was all excited and nervous, whereas I was calm and not at all alarmed. As I am frightened of practically everything, such as speech-making—sailing—animals—parties—the dark and lonely lane—why am I not alarmed at functions which seem to frighten quite a lot of people?'

CHAPTER X

Private Affairs, 1919–1939

From the preceding chapters it might well be thought that Trudie's life was one of all work and no play, and that neglect of home and children must have been the penalty for all the public activities which she felt compelled to undertake because, as she once wrote to a friend, 'there are such lots of things that are so untidy and I get fussy and feel something should be done about them.' But nothing was, in fact, further from the truth. Trudie had the great gift of being able, at will, to put aside public cares and responsibilities. Week-end visitors to Balcombe—generally a few old friends—found nothing to remind them of their gay and relaxed hostess's public importance. Talk was easy and general. It was never 'highbrow', although her practical and humorous approach salted all the topics of the day. Her own special cares and interests were seldom, if ever, mentioned. The same carefree spirit prevailed when, as in most years, she went on holiday in February to the South of France with two or three friends to play golf and tennis. 'Now we're off,' she would exclaim as the train pulled out of Victoria Station; and from that moment public worries were cast away.

Games continued to be Trudie's great joy and relaxation. She was an indefatigably keen and sporting player, always generous whether she lost or won, and always an encouraging partner. Golf and tennis came first in importance. At neither was she an outstanding performer, though above average, especially at tennis where she was aided by a good eye and by fleetness of foot. The grass courts at Balcombe were kept up to Wimbledon standard. Trudie would herself eradicate weeds, roll the lawn and apply lawn-sand. In summer she organized many tennis week-ends, skilfully managing both the experts and the young people whom she invited as company for her own children, so that everyone enjoyed a good game. Each year she would devote a week to playing in the East Grinstead County tournament for which she practised assiduously. At golf she often played in matches for the Ladies' Parliamentary Golf Association, and she was a regular player on the Haywards Heath and Ashdown Forest courses. There was golf, too, at Aldeburgh on the Suffolk coast, within easy reach of the villa on the edge of the sea at Thorpeness, which Trudie and her sister-in-law, Alicia, bought in 1933 as a holiday house for themselves, their grandchildren and their friends. With two highly competent elderly retainers as its resident staff, the little Thorpeness house provided the nicest kind of simple comfort with an atmosphere of real holiday relaxation.

Nor did Trudie ever allow her public work to come between her and her two children, Thomas and Judith. Having suffered herself from a sometimes lonely childhood, she managed to devote much more time to her children than did many contemporary mothers whose engagements were mainly of a social character. 'Shop' was never talked at home. Occasionally her children might hear a grumble that someone or something had been tiresome. Occasionally they would be told not to talk too much because someone was coming to lunch to discuss business. The only time, indeed, that her family were really conscious of her public work was when an atmosphere of strain would build up during the two or three days before the Women's Institutes' Annual General Meeting. Even then there would be no hurry or last minute preparations. Her speech would have been written and mulled over days before. But, to her own annoyance, since she had presided there so often, Trudie could never calmly face the ordeal of the great Albert Hall gathering.

Her ideas on the upbringing of children were in advance of her day. She believed in treating them as intelligent beings, who would respond more readily to reason and example than to punishment. Neither at Balcombe, nor at 43 Upper Grosvenor Street, was there a schoolroom in which to isolate the children. Instead, as soon as they left the nursery, they had meals with their parents. To her children, Trudie seemed to have infinite leisure for companionship, for reading aloud and playing card games, for cutting down trees and bushes and building bonfires, and for helping them to learn tennis and golf and to ride and swim. In the Christmas holidays of 1921 and 1922 she took the children to Mürren for winter sports. With them, she enjoyed the skating and ski-ing. Finding to her annoyance that, although there was the Kandahar Cup for male skiers, there was no trophy for women, she presented the Denman Cup for the latter. The Society papers noted that Lady Denman pioneered the sensible fashion of wearing breeches instead of skirts. During their second visit to Mürren several visitors, including Thomas and Judith, developed scarlet fever. Wishing to be with and help nurse her children instead of having them removed to the isolation hospital, Trudie organized the lease of a villa jointly with other patients and their relatives. Soon, however, she herself caught the infection. The Swiss quarantine was six weeks against the English four, so Trudie was faced with remaining in Switzerland for two weeks after they could have all returned home out of quarantine. Determined to avoid this, she kept her own scarlet fever dark, but she realized that she must find some excuse for staying in bed. She therefore made a resounding noise by slipping down the stairs with a jug of water, got into bed, summoned the doctor, cautiously showed him a knee professedly inflamed by her fall and obtained his orders to lie up and rest her leg. At the end of four weeks they all travelled home together.

There were summer holidays, too, to share with the children. One year they visited friends at Bembridge in the Isle of Wight, but usually they all went to Dunecht, the great estate of farmland, forest and moor with its huge Italianate palace, which Lord Cowdray had bought from Lord Crawford and Balcarres. There Trudie taught the children golf, fished and went for picnics. She did not like or take part in the shooting. As the children grew older, Trudie organized many parties of young people for them at Balcombe. Here, from a letter to her son, is her description of one such party in January 1927. Even in her forties, she could still enter into all the fun.

'The dance was a huge success. A very nice energetic party. We played hockey against Arundel and got beaten (only just) because they played without rules and it took us some time to realize that we could barge people and trip them up, lock their sticks, shoot goals from the middle of the ground and remain offside indefinitely. In our attempt to be as rough as they were, most of us had injuries, but we think we gave them a few blows to remember too! We also had charades and I was allowed to be the drunken waiter, so you see I had several treats.'

Her son's education had to follow the conventional lines of preparatory boarding school, Eton and Cambridge. But she took a special interest in her daughter's schooling, sending her first, unconventionally, to a mixed Froebel Institute in West Kensington, and later, after discarding a French governess, to boarding school at Ascot, before keeping her at home in London under a tutor in order to enter Cambridge to take an engineering degree. In 1926, Trudie went with Judith to Newnham to see her settled in to her new Cambridge life. The letter she wrote her next day shows the relationship established between mother and daughter.

'It was terribly sad leaving you yesterday, and all the way home, or at least half the way home, I thought how much I should miss you. There is no doubt about it, you are a very nice child to have; you don't neglect me and you always come and talk to me, and yet at the same time I never feel you are on my hands and want amusing. You laugh at my jokes and tell me all (or most of) the news and what you are thinking. So it is not to be wondered at that I hate your being away. . . . One thing is that you will become as thin as a rail if the meals are no more tempting than the dinner was. . . . Don't be too hardy, but think of all the men living in the lap of luxury, and get all the comfort you can. If you lunch out each day and take one other with you, then at least there will be two girls not starving!'

Trudie again stayed with Judith at Cambridge before her final examinations. Much as she disliked social life, she also brought her daughter out for two conventional London seasons before Cambridge. The late nights and trying to stay awake were a particular agony to her!

Until the beginning of the Second World War, Lord Denman continued to make his home at Balcombe and at 43 Upper Grosvenor Street. He was, however, abroad for many months each year in winter to avoid bronchitis, and in summer to escape hay fever. Even when at home, he was often ill. Trudie and he had succeeded in building up a relationship which preserved outward appearances. They often played golf and tennis together, and their relationship contained kindness and tolerance, Denman continuing to turn to his wife for practical help in all matters, but it afforded Trudie no real companionship. Denman's own career had never fulfilled its early promise. This was due in part to the unwavering loyalty with which he supported the 'Wee Free' or Asquithian Liberals. In 1923 he became their chief whip in the House of Lords and was in the Party's inner councils with such colleagues as Lord Crewe and Lord Grey of Fallodon. He spoke in the Lords in opposition to the Coalition Government's policies in Ireland and over its handling of industrial unrest at home, as well as taking a special interest in Australia and other Commonwealth questions. But after 1924, when he gave up being Chief Whip, he devoted himself increasingly to the care of his health, although he continued to attend the House of Lords and was a deputy speaker there for some thirty years. For a few years after 1919, he trained his own steeplechase horses, sometimes riding them in races for amateur riders, and became a Steward of National Hunt Racing. He won his last race in 1924 at the age of 50 and then gave up his horses.

Apart from her children and from members of the Pearson clan—her ties with her brother Clive and his wife were always particularly strong—Trudie found companionship and affection in a few close friends. Of these, perhaps the most important was Neville Lytton, the artist. He had been one of the first visitors at Balcombe in 1906 and, after the war, constantly stayed there, as well as, in several years, forming one of the happy golf and tennis party in the South of France. Excelling at games, witty and light-hearted, unorthodox and outspoken, Neville's company was a special delight for Trudie. As an artist he was a traditionalist. It was through his influence and in helping forward his career that

Trudie acquired an interest in painting. The friendship was mutually treasured, Neville Lytton once writing to her,

> 'I can't remember in all the course of our friendship your ever saying or doing anything that did not seem to me generous, chivalrous and large-hearted; and you are as fundamentally good as you are fundamentally wise. I am deeply grateful for what you have done for me artistically, and I am still more grateful for your example in *everything*.'

Another early and close friendship which continued unweakened through the years was that with Nellie Grant, who made Balcombe her headquarters whenever she came back from Kenya for a visit to England. It was through her that, in the thirties, her daughter and son-in-law joined the small circle of regular visitors to Balcombe and Thorpeness. Trudie's friendship with Lady Sanderson dated from Australian days. She and another old friend, Lord Charles Hope, both very good games players, usually helped to make up the party for the Riviera holiday each winter and were much at Balcombe. Trudie's Presidency of the Ladies' Golf Union brought her another devoted games-playing friend in Joy Winn, the golf international. Susan Ertz, the novelist, was a close friend whom Trudie acquired in the early nineteen-twenties, and, from 1933, Margaret Pyke became a frequent visitor to Balcombe.

Trudie did not wear her heart on her sleeve, but to her friends she was warmly and deeply affectionate. She had the faculty of making those around her come up to their best form, and her love of laughter made her company a particular joy. But what was more important was that pettiness and pretence could not exist in the direct and transparent honesty and generosity of her presence. As Neville Lytton had written, her example, even more than the help and advice freely given over problems great and small, exercised a lasting influence over the lives of all those who were fortunate enough to enjoy her friendship.

Neither Trudie's public activities nor her week-ends of relaxation with her family and friends would have been possible unless she had been free from household chores. Like her father, she had the power of delegation. For her household's administration, she chose her senior employees well, gave them clear general instructions, and left all the details at Balcombe and Upper Grosvenor Street in their competent hands. All four members of this senior group had been in her service for many years. They were devoted to her and lived up to their responsibilities, appreciating and responding to the trust which allowed them each to run his or her department without interference. There was Andrews the butler who had been first engaged as Lord Denman's valet and who had gone to Australia with him, before becoming butler at Government House and returning to England with the family to continue to serve as their butler. Under Andrews and his satellite footmen the households ran with smooth and unobtrusive efficiency. The kitchen and catering department was in charge of an equally trusted employee, 'Mrs' Missenden, who had entered Trudie's service in 1914. Trudie hated elaborate meals, but enjoyed good food, especially that prepared by Mrs Missenden in whom she had such complete confidence that she seldom looked at the menus beforehand, although her standards were high and she always noticed any lapse. 'So and so was not quite as nice as usual,' she would say to Mrs Missenden on such rare occasions; but she always remembered to praise any special dish or effort. Then, there was Miss Young, Trudie's personal maid since her return from Australia in 1914. Trudie herself was not interested in dress. Her own preference was for her old country clothes, her 'grubbing clothes' as she called them. But she liked to be suitably dressed, and her clothes, bought from Reville, were of the best quality though simple. She took special trouble over her hunting kit and the dresses she wore for important events such as the Women's Institutes' Annual General Meeting or the Ladies' Golf Union's annual dinner, when she felt that she owed it to the occasion to be as smart as possible, with her red-gold hair specially waved. She was no needlewoman and once said to Young, 'If I had to make my own nighties, I wouldn't wear them. I'd just have one by my bedside in case of fire.' With Miss Young in charge, however, Trudie had no need to occupy her time and her mind over matters of clothes. The fourth of the group of senior servants was her chauffeur, Ashford. When he died, his place was taken by the equally devoted and efficient Burnett. Trudie was also able to rely on Mrs Molesworth, her part-time secretary for many years. It was still considered ill-mannered to type personal letters such as invitations to stay, and it was of particular advantage that Mrs Molesworth's handwriting so resembled Trudie's as to be almost indistinguishable.

Trudie's punctuality was one of her great assets as an employer. Mrs Missenden boasted that she never served a meal late in thirty years. An equal asset was that she was always straight, frank and entirely just. She earned the respect of those who served her, as well as winning their affection through her friendly and easy manner and her consideration for their welfare. She kept a watchful eye on the well-being of the junior servants, on whose behalf she was always on the side of leniency. At Balcombe the senior domestic staff had the use of a hard tennis court, and Trudie and her tennis playing friends would sometimes join their games.

Many years before, when she was in Canada on her way back to Australia, Trudie had written to her brother Clive that, 'If I must be civilized, I do like to be comfortable and have the best of everything. What I would like best would be to have a ranch or something and be quite uncivilized, but what I do hate is dirty indifferent civilization.' It was this civilized comfort, of the best but simple and free from any hint of fussy ostentation, that Trudie achieved in her households. But even though she was free from domestic worries, she would never have managed to get so much done unless she had kept to a regular routine. The early part of the morning was always devoted to her work. Her breakfast was brought to her in bed every morning at eight with her letters, and she would do much of the business of the day before she came downstairs. Sometimes, when the pressure on her was heavy, she would work for an hour or more before breakfast.

Besides relaxation, Trudie had responsibilities at Balcombe. There was the management of the estate with its fifteen tenant farmers, its woodlands and its cottages. An estate agent was shared between Balcombe and Paddockhurst. Trudie took her landlord's duties seriously, insisting on being kept fully informed and meeting her agent in regular session. She took great interest in questions of forestry; and, since she hated to think of housewives and mothers deprived of the help of modern conveniences, she paid special attention to the provision of electricity, bathrooms, and water-closets for the cottages she owned. But she was no farmer, and her personal interest did not extend either to the running of the home farm with its dairy herd, or to the agricultural problems of her tenant farmers. Building was, however something that she understood and enjoyed. It was in her blood. She acted as her own architect in the alterations which were made to Balcombe in 1919. She also herself drew up the plans and supervised the alterations to Brantridge Park before the Earl of Athlone and Princess Alice became her tenants there. Her father contributed £10,000 towards the cost. He wanted her to employ an architect and rebuild the whole place, but Trudie was firm in her resolve to preserve the house and to be herself responsible for its improvement.

With her Clerk of the Works, she designed and built a new block of cottages, as well as the Balcombe Victory Hall, a Community Centre for the village, to be managed by the Men's Club and the Women's Institute. The chief feature of the Hall was a pair of frescoes, each thirty-four feet long by ten feet high, which Trudie commissioned Neville Lytton to execute. They were true frescoes, painted by the artist on to the wet plaster with colours mixed with ten-year lime. Their subjects were War and Peace. Neville Lytton wrote to Trudie to say, 'I can't tell you how satisfactory it is to do a decoration for a definite spot and to finish it "en place", as in the days of the great renaissance.' The frescoes aroused a good deal of interest when the Hall was opened in 1925, and the art critics of *The Times*, *Daily Telegraph* and *Daily Mail* devoted considerable space to favourable comment on them. In gratitude for Trudie's contribution in time and money, the village Committee presented her with a key to the Hall so that it 'would always be open to her and her husband'. The organization and finance of the Hall remained one of Trudie's local concerns, as did the Balcombe Women's Institute which had been started in 1917 with Trudie as President.

There was one branch of local affairs in which Trudie took little part. This was the Church. Lady Cowdray was a devout churchwoman and had brought her children up in her beliefs. Trudie had been confirmed in Westminster Abbey, but as she grew to maturity and thought things out for herself, she found that dogma and the outward forms of religion meant nothing to her. What mattered to her was individual behaviour, and she observed that many churchgoers signally failed, to her way of thinking, to live up to Christian standards. She ceased to be a regular churchgoer, saying that church so often left her feeling cross and frustrated, the more since she was unable to argue with the preacher when she could not accept all that he said from the pulpit. When reading Kingsley's *Water Babies* aloud to her children, she had impressed on them that 'Do as you would be done by' was the most important precept for them to observe. It summed up her own transparent goodness and her high ethical standards.

Trudie had no special bent for literature, but she had read widely in her youth and she continued to be much better read than she gave herself out to be. It was, however, mainly through her friends that she acquired her appreciation for the arts. Neville Lytton liked to discuss books and poetry with her. In sending her a copy of the collected poems of his father-in-law, Wilfred Scawen Blunt, he wrote in the fly-leaf,

> 'My father-in-law was in a certain sense a pupil of my father, and to the same extent I am a pupil of Wilfred Blunt. That being so, my admiration of these verses may come from a sort of filial piety (once removed). You, who have discretion and judgement in all things, will be able to tell me whether this is living poetry.'

Margaret Pyke was another friend whose cultural background Trudie enjoyed contrasting with her own non-academic up-bringing. 'I have often wondered what kind of people won these competitions,' she wrote to congratulate Margaret on winning a literary competition in *Time and Tide*. 'I thought that they must really be people like the Master of Balliol, Virginia Woolf and

Keynes. I am very proud to think that now I know one of these marvellous beings.'

Her own special interest was in old furniture. Here, her knowledge, taste and judgement were so good that, after her death, the experts from the Victoria and Albert Museum classed all the furniture she had collected for her bedroom as museum pieces. Through Lady Sanderson she tried to gain an appreciation of music, and, as we have seen, it was Neville Lytton who aroused her interest in pictures.

One February—it was in 1929—she visited Italy with her sister-in-law and closest friend, Alicia Pearson, an exceptionally widely-read connoisseur of the Arts. Trudie designed the expedition as a means of helping her sister-in-law to recover from the great strain of nursing her mother through her last illness. Her own appetite for Italy had been sharpened by a previous visit, a few years earlier, when she had hired a car and taken Judith and Lady Sanderson to Florence and Venice, returning home by Munich and Hanover.

Trudie and Alicia kept a joint diary of their tour. Their sight-seeing was seriously and indefatigably pursued in spite of bitterly cold weather and unheated galleries, which led to such entries in the diary as, 'we went to the first floor and stood in a patch of sunlight, trying to enjoy seeing the Dying Gladiator, but all we could think of was the awful cold.'

The travellers spent a strenuous fortnight in Rome, and then went on to Siena and Florence for ten equally crowded days. On the whole it was the architecture that most aroused Trudie's critical and practical interest. 'In Rome,' she wrote in the diary, 'it is the small things which I like—the doors and window frames in the courtyard [at the Castel San Angelo] are perfection, small, plain and neat; every cottage should have door frames just like these.' Or, visiting the Lateran Museum, 'the sculpture is not very beautiful, but there are friezes and cornices and columns and pillars, table legs and bowls and urns that an architect could study for weeks and that abound in perfect designs.' She found the Colosseum impressive from the outside, 'but inside one just gets a gloomy picture of martyrs, gladiators and animals, all fighting

Family Group at Cowdray, 1919

Left to right, back row: Mrs Kinnell, Lord Denman, Miss Baba Kinnell, Lord Cowdray, Harold Pearson. *Seated centre*: Beryl Pearson, Lady Cowdray, Joan Pearson, Trudie Pearson, *Standing on right*: Nancy Pearson, Bishop Brown

In front: Thomas Denman, Judith Denman, Yoskil, Brenda, John and Angela Pearson

for their lives;' and the Pantheon struck her 'as a most dour spot. I have seldom seen a building with less to recommend it. It even smelled most unpleasantly.' It was to the Vatican that they went again and again, 'revelling in the Fra Angelico Chapel', whose 'purity and severity always makes me want to go home and at once start to lead an austere and saintly life. I must see its gentleness again before the eye and mind are overwhelmed by the Michel Angelo paintings in the Sistine Chapel. The panel showing man touching the finger of God is the most perfect design. If only one could lie in a hammock and enjoy gazing at the paintings in comfort.' Siena was terribly cold; 'lovely early pictures with golden backgrounds [in the Accademia dei Belle Arte] but the gallery so icy that our appreciation froze.' Florence, however, was sunny, and, on arrival, they were 'up earlier than usual from excitement and had a very pleasant morning revisiting all the lovely things we knew.'

Neville Lytton once wrote to Trudie that 'the sight of a rich woman going through the eye of a needle is so rare, that that alone is a matter for wonder, but your incredible unselfishness to everyone on every occasion is something that I have never met with before.' Thanks to her father's ability, enterprise and labours, she was an extremely wealthy woman, but the pursuit of money, *qua* money, held no interest for her. Money, to her, was useful in that it allowed her to live in comfort, to enjoy the simple pleasures of her choice, and to devote herself to causes in which she believed; it was important in that it enabled her to support such causes with generous financial help, and readily to assist friends in need. This private generosity to friends was always astonishingly thoughtful, discriminating and warm-hearted. Through it she gave unexpected but invaluable help to many when it was most wanted. But never did any rich person carry about her less of the aura of money; and she took care to keep her children in their youth ignorant of their probable future wealth. Riches, she felt, carried with them the responsibility for their wise and careful use. Always grudging spending anything on herself, she strongly disliked any form of extravagance or ostentation, and firmly resisted her mother's efforts to persuade her to live on a grander social scale, such as owning a yacht or a racing stable. Owing to her prudent care, she was able, during the twenties and thirties, to save a large sum from her income. This stood her in good stead in the war years and after, when taxation rose to 19s. 6d. in the £, enabling her to meet the increasing costs of Balcombe and to maintain some of the generosity of her help to others.

The year 1927 brought Trudie two great sorrows. One was the death of her father, Lord Cowdray. He and Lady Cowdray had been given the Freedom of the City of Aberdeen. At the end of April Trudie and her brother Harold travelled to Dunecht to be with their parents for the ceremony. They found Lord Cowdray looking in better health than for some time past. In the afternoon, in happy mood, he read his speech to the family circle. But in the evening he felt ill, and he died in the night, practically in his sleep. The love, trust and pride in each other's achievements shared between Trudie and her father had been very great. His sudden death at seventy-one was a tragic blow. It came, too, at a moment when she had need of all his sympathy and support to help her sustain the greater tragedy which now encompassed her. The bond with her son Thomas had always been of the closest. She was devoted to him and intensely proud of his successes, such as his membership of the School Shooting VIII at Eton. He loved pictures, poetry and books, and adored his mother. But, since adolescence, relationships with others seemed to have become increasingly difficult for him, although Trudie exercised all her love and protection to try to help him. The year before, when he was 21 and in his last year at Cambridge, he had virtually cut himself off from his friends to retire into his own shell. A voyage to Chile that winter with his uncle and aunt, the Clive Pearsons, had been of no avail. Now, in the summer of 1927, the haunting shadow of her son's complete estrangement from her became a reality; and, as time went on, bitter as it was for Trudie to accept, it became clear that, for his own well-being, he must live in the isolation of a world of his own making, cut off from his family and the real world outside. The tragedy was made harder to bear by the general lack of understanding of mental cases, but Trudie's abiding grief was shouldered with all her courage and fortitude. It was privately borne and was never allowed to obtrude on her friends or outwardly to affect her life and work.

Lady Cowdray died in 1932. Her death took place in Paris, where Trudie went to be with her in her last days. Annie's love for her daughter had been genuine and she took great pride in her achievements. But she had never understood her and had continued to be critical of her friends, her clothes and her values, so that there was always some constraint between them. Nevertheless, her mother's death left a gap in Trudie's life and broke yet another link with her father and the past.

But the thirties also brought Trudie much family happiness through the marriage of Judith in 1931 to Walter Burrell, the son of a Sussex neighbour, and, in the years that followed, through the birth of four grandchildren. Trudie insisted on all the children being born at 43 Upper Grosvenor Street, in order that she could see that her daughter was properly looked after. She much enjoyed being a grandmother, and in Penelope, her eldest grandchild, she found someone to replace her lost son in her affection. Children always liked Trudie. They found her such fun to be with, and she seemed to like the things that they themselves liked best, such as games and picnics and dressing up.

Trudie had always enjoyed the robust health needed to support, without overstrain, the intense activity of the life she led. But in the early months of 1936, when she was 51, her constitution was to be gravely weakened. In mid-February she and Margaret Pyke had gone on a golfing holiday to join Lord Denman at Valescure on the Riviera. There, without warning, Trudie developed acute appendicitis. Mismanagement by the French doctors and nurses led to peritonitis and acute intestinal obstruction. In those days before penicillin, there seemed to be little hope of saving her life. Her daughter and her brother Clive and his wife flew out to be with her. After days of anxiety they summoned Mr Arthur Evans, the London surgeon, who later also called in Sir Adolphe Abrahams from London. Dr Evans had to conduct two operations, the first lasting more than three hours. Against his expectations she began to recover, thanks to the combination of his skill and her vitality, which he compared to that of a youth of 21. 'What a good advertisement for smoking and drinking too much,' was her subsequent comment. She bore intense pain with great fortitude, insisting that her daughter's recent experience of giving birth to twins must have been much worse. Afterwards she was much concerned at the expense her illness was causing. 'I doubt if I shall ever justify all that you have spent on me,' she was heard to murmur. A little later, when she was convalescent, she declared herself consoled because, when some papers came to her from the Land Settlement Association with plans for the cottages they were building, she saw that only outside lavatories had been provided. She successfully insisted on indoor lavatories being built, pointing out that, owing to the need to visit an outside lavatory, mortality from pneumonia was greater in the 'healthy' countryside than it was in the slums. Her life, she felt, had not been prolonged in vain!

It was not until May that she was able to be moved back to England on a stretcher, and when she got home she had to undergo a further operation. Midsummer was past before she was up and about again. Meantime, the news of her critical illness had caused consternation to her friends and to her colleagues in the Institutes and other organizations which she served. Newspapers commented that 'an army of women are offering up sincere good wishes for her speedy and complete recovery', and a flood of letters reached her from individual Institutes and from County Federations, while her presence was sadly missed at the Institutes' Annual General Meeting. Miss Hadow, who deputized for her, wrote from Oxford, 'I can think of no one outside Royalty—and major Royalty at that!—about whom so many people would be so genuinely and warmly concerned'; and a member of the Executive wrote to tell her how the Vice-Chairmen were 'replete with impartiality, but, my Lord, they *do* make things so dull.' From the Family Planning Association, her friend Mark Grant-Sturgis sent her long and amusing letters about the progress of the Gala Ballet at Sadlers Wells which he was helping to organize on behalf of the Association's funds. 'Of course,' he wrote, 'what we really want is a Birth Control Ballet with you and D [Lord

Skating at Mürren with Thomas and Judith, 1921

Recruiting for Land
Army, 1917

With Neville Lytton
at a lawn-tennis tournament,
St Cloud, 1920

Denman] doing the Markova and Dolin stuff, and all the corps
de ballet as quads and quints.'

Trudie's physical resources never fully recovered from the
1936 crisis. From then on she lived with digestion much impaired
and severed stomach muscles. At first she took things more easily,
but this irked her and, before long, her life was as active as
ever.

One further private event of the nineteen-thirties remains to
be chronicled. It was a visit to Kenya which she made in the
winter of 1930-1931 to stay with Nellie Grant. She kept a full diary
of this exciting break in her routine. It is written with refreshing
objectivity, and it reveals so well the essential Trudie with all her
simplicity and sense of fun, that the story of the Kenya interlude,
based on the diary, must have a chapter to itself.

CHAPTER XI

Kenya Interlude

Accompanied by Judith, her twenty-three-year-old daughter who had just left Cambridge, and by Miss Young her personal maid, Trudie left England at the end of November 1930 on a German liner. At Genoa they met Trudie's niece, Yoskyl Pearson, who was on her way to stay with friends in Cairo. With her daughter, Trudie went 'in a rich car' to see the sights of Genoa.

'The cemetery was incredible,' she recorded in her diary, 'rows of tombs and monuments for miles on the side of a hill and at the foot. Not a square inch wasted. Judy and I didn't look at it for long, such overcrowding made it seem too unhygienic, and we imagined or smelled a nasty odour of decay. Yoskyl in the morning had discovered some treasures, including one monument containing a statue of a gentleman in a bowler hat being raised up to Heaven by an angel holding him up by his whiskers. I talked to our German Captain about this at our first meal after leaving Genoa. I said that in America also they had rich tombs, but that in England—and was I not right in saying in Germany too?—the monuments to the dead were more simple. "No," said the German Captain indignantly, "We, too, in Germany have very rich tombs!" He would not have the Fatherland insulted.'

The party soon settled into ship-board routine with its gossip and rumours about the other passengers. 'It is strange how much less exciting people are when you talk to them instead of looking at them from far off and inventing romantic stories about them,' Trudie commented. Deck games started, 'I beat both Yoskyl and Judy at deck tennis which I have never played before. I am pleased about this, as I think it shows there is life in the old dog yet.' Trudie also tried some serious reading. 'Between tea and dinner, when it is too dark for games, I have read *Points of View* to Judy who is knitting a very loud pair of stockings. Wells's ideas on individuality and the place of man in the universe caused Yoskyl to say "Gosh" twice, while Judy murmured at intervals "I do like being read to while I knit"; but in spite of these signs of appreciation, I don't feel so far that our readings have had a very stimulating effect on our intellectual growth.'

From Port Said, the party visited Cairo. At Cook's office Trudie 'refused to pay £7 a head which is the inclusive fare for the trip and just paid for a car to Cairo, a jaunt to the Pyramids and the tickets back to Suez. This came to £19 instead of £28, so I saved a bit by being firm.'

She was not impressed by the Egyptian Scene—

'Very dirty men all with long robes like nightgowns trailing in the dust; women all in black (filthy). The bullocks were thin with such high withers that they looked like emaciated bison; camels all flea-bitten and miserable; donkeys so small that we could hardly see them for the bundles or the men they were carrying. At least 30% of the cars we passed had broken down and were being pushed along, and the others generally had 6 or 7 inside and sometimes another 6 on the running board and luggage rack. Just as the sordidness of the drive became almost unbearable, we got to Cairo with its broad streets, gardens with palms and modern Parisian buildings.'

In Cairo, Yoskyl was met by her friends and left the party, while Trudie, Judy and Miss Young went off to see the Pyramids.

'Our dragoman asked us if we would go round the Pyramids by sand-cart, donkey or camel. I firmly chose the last, and when we arrived we picked three camels which were surprisingly clean and very amenable. Yoskyl had frightened us by saying that camels, when annoyed, spit at you and that their spit consists of maggots! I was therefore very polite to my camel and said "What a lovely camel" in my slow clear English which I reserve for foreigners. This had the desired effect and my camel was very gentle. The Pyramids reminded me very much of the wall part of the rock garden, except that the rocks looked to be about 10 foot by 6 foot. The sphinx is quite close and we rode round that too. Our dragoman told us a great deal which I couldn't understand, but our three camels stood facing him in a most attentive manner and seemed to be drinking in every word.'

After leaving Suez, Trudie wrote that

'life on board ship has gone peacefully ahead. We had sports yesterday and Judy was placed in 3 events. I restrained myself from entering, as I thought it wasn't seemly. When I get back, I must have my face lifted so that I shall look young enough to compete in potato races and all the things I really enjoy.'

When they left Aden, they ran into bad weather.

'Although we are coasting down the East of Africa it has rained ever since two o'clock today. I didn't get my usual sleep this afternoon as it was not only raining but foggy, and I kept awake in case we ran into anything and had to take to the boats. I prepared my overcoat putting in the pockets—brandy, Mothersill, cigarettes, matches, a tube of lanoline, also my note case. I thought the latter might be useful if and when we got ashore!!'

The Fancy Dress Dance took place the next evening. Trudie at first,

'said haughtily that I had dressed up for 40 years and was not taking part tonight. At tea time I suggested that Young should go as a golfer. She was rather lukewarm about it, so I said I would go as her caddy. I didn't dress until after dinner and am now sitting writing got up as follows—a large check cap; cigarette behind ear; black round the jaw; dirty muffler; waistcoat with button off; trousers with two patches; socks hanging down over dirty tennis shoes; an enormous bag of clubs and a rag to polish clubs and clean the ball. Young as Miss Cecil Leitch was superb, tall and hefty and dignified, with collar and tie and golfing shoes of sturdy build. I think we were a popular if undignified turn. Dash—the fog must be bad again; they are blowing the fog horn and letting off lights or rockets. If we did run into anything, we should be a low looking crowd if we were rescued by a passing steamer. I have just washed my face as I should so hate to be put in the steerage! But I am not going to change my trousers as they make me feel very brave. Supper has just been served but the dressing up spirit has died in me; at the same time I am very hungry. I shall go and find Judy and get her to hand me a bun. Later, I have just had a very good supper and hear that I have won first prize—given by vote—for my costume.'

The next day Trudie fancied that she 'got rather a cold look from a prim old maid called Miss Whitehead whose parents were friends of the family about forty years ago. I was told that when someone asked her if she didn't think I was the best, she replied, "Not at all, *much* too realistic and not at all suitable for a lady!!!"'

Mombasa was reached on December 17th and, after a drive round Mombasa island, Trudie and her party took the afternoon train for Nairobi. Next morning,

'I woke Judy up at 5 as we were in the Game Reserve and we sat from then till 10 with our eyes glued to the window excepting only for the moments when we washed our respective faces. We saw 2 giraffes, ostriches by the dozen, zebra and about 4 different kinds of buck.'

Nellie Grant was at the station at Nairobi to meet them and took them off to the Muthaiga Club for the night. It was arranged that Miss Young should stay there while Nellie took Trudie and Judy up country to her farm at Njoro. Nellie 'introduced my new maid to me, a black gentleman with an enormous mouth and a red turban.'

Trudie much enjoyed next day's 120-mile drive to Njoro over the escarpment with its stupendous view of the Rift Valley. In her diary she particularly noted the wild flowers and the lovely birds of all colours, including a 'tiny bird which looks like a small purple plum with a lovely bloom on it.' Finally, as their car climbed the hill from Njoro,

'round a corner we came on lovely flower borders, a blaze of colour—hollyhocks, carnations, every kind of lily, and hiding behind them a series of little houses made of mud covered with white plaster and a tin roof. And this was Nellie's house. It doesn't look very grand from the outside, but inside it is lovely. All small rooms, but lovely comfy chairs and beds and a bathroom for me next my bedroom and 3 others as well! I think it is a record for the size of the house.'

The next morning Trudie woke up to a 'wonderful sunrise' and 'an amazingly beautiful view' out of her window, over the Rift Valley and Lake Nakuru, with the blue Aberdare mountains in the far distance. 'Dressed up in jodhpurs and my top with pockets and felt very grand.'

After a golf-match in which Trudie and Nellie played for Njoro against Nakuru, Trudie 'packed for our week's safari, feeling very apprehensive of motoring miles through deserted country crawling with wild animals.'

Their first day's camp was in an uninhabited house about sixty miles from Thomson's Falls. They had a picnic lunch and looked at the Falls 'which were very fine, but half my mind was wondering if the lorry and its black driver in plus-fours with my maid and the cook on the front seat and the parlour maid and kitchen maid balanced on top of the load would turn up before it got dark!' All was, however, well, and they reached camp after driving for miles along 'a bumpy track which was so overgrown with coarse grass that it was hard to tell how deep the ruts were'; and 'I had a lovely time making a fire with chips and odd bits whilst the camp was being unpacked. A good dinner, eggs, bacon and sausages and a glass of beer.'

After an early start next morning, they spent several hours losing their way over rough trails across the plain until they found the main road—

'not much better than the track—and passed every kind of buck and ostriches, and Judy and Jos [Nellie's husband, Major Josceline Grant] who were in front saw zebra and wild pig. All this was very exciting, but I didn't much like the idea of camping at night. I have almost been persuaded that lions, provided there are fires, run away at once, but Jos will tell me tactless stories about rhinos charging motor-cars and knocking them endways.'

However, they got safely to Nanyuki, seventy miles away for lunch at the hotel, 'a very nice group of thatched buildings round a lawn. Each building was a bedroom and very clean and nice. There was a notice up saying that it was a wonderful centre for seeing rhinos, lions etc. etc. and for trout fishing! On reading this I suggested that it would be lovely to sleep in one of the dear little huts and have a comfy bath and an afternoon's fishing. The others fell in with my cowardly suggestion.'

The next day, Christmas Eve, they drove sixty miles round the foot of Mount Kenya to Meru, where they stayed in the Game Warden's house. There they spent Christmas, playing 'crossword games, noun game and book consequences, all new to Nellie.'

On Boxing Day, the party set off for Embu, some hundred miles away along

'a wonderful road winding round the foothills; brilliant green vegetation, banana trees and palms and every sort of flowering bushes. Coming slowly round one corner over a bridge crossing a little river, we saw Judy peering over the side and several people doing likewise. We then saw that our lorry had missed the bridge, skidded down a bank and turned on its side with its bonnet in the river. Nobody was hurt at all, the parlour maids etc. who travel on top of the lorry had jumped clear, including the driver which was very clever of him. I suggested weakly to Nellie that we should abandon the lorry and go on ourselves in the other 2 cars. No, Nellie said, she would get it pulled out. I suggested that wouldn't help as we couldn't tow the thing round those nasty corners with the steering gear probably not working. I didn't press the point, as I am a parcel and am doing what I am told to do quite nicely I think. However Nellie went off to collect some black gentlemen to help and returned with about 8 in her car and another dozen coming along as fast as they could. They got ropes tied on and pulled the lorry back on to its paws. They then cut a bush or two and 20 to 30 men on each of the two ropes sang a song which means "We are men not children" and three good heaves got the lorry up the bank and on to the road. We then counted our army of helpers and found there were 48. Between us we raised 32 shilling pieces which we handed round and gave bits of paper to the remaining 16 helpers, explaining that the headman would pay a shilling to each later on when he had change. This created a tremendous stir, shoutings and gesticulations and no amount of explanations soothed them. We heard there was a shop 3 miles on, so Judy and I stepped into a car to go and see. All the unpaid workers wanted to come with us. Two managed to get in but Judy got away before the back of the car was rushed. Judy tootled round a hairpin bend which frightened another car so much that, in avoiding us, it went into the ditch. By then we were pretty good at pushing cars, so we soon got that one on the road again and moreover got 5/- change from the occupants. The native bazaar had no money, but a picnic party had, so we turned round to go back to the others and met Nellie driving the lorry in triumph with the crestfallen driver beside her. We continued on our curly road—I believe we crossed 80 culverts all told—and got to Embu in good time to camp. We had lovely bacon and eggs and my trout all fried up together with taters. A fine camp fire and we opened a new bottle of gin. A most pleasant evening.'

The next day, the party reached Nyeri for a 'superb breakfast' at the Outspan hotel, after losing Jos who had two punctures and came in on the rim two hours later. Then home to Njoro via Thomson's Falls and Gil Gil. 'I have never been so dirty as when we arrived at 9.30. We were bumping along in the cars for 12 hours out of 15, but I don't think any of us were tired.'

After a few more days at Njoro, Nellie took Trudie and Judy down to Nairobi for the 'race week, a terrific affair'. They stayed, very comfortably, at Lady MacMillan's large house, with Miss Young to look after Trudie again. At the races Trudie made 6s. on the day. 'In this country,' she commented, 'pounds don't exist so one writes cheques for thousands of shillings which seems most extravagant.' Trudie played golf and watched the polo matches in which Nellie played back for her team. There were dinner parties every night, and Trudie 'survived till 2.30 a.m.'. During the week she met Lord Delamere and all the Kenya celebrities, and 'Mr Moore, the acting Governor told me so much about native administration that I am completely muddled but very interested.'

'It was very nice to get home to Njoro again,' Trudie recorded, 'to peace and quiet; Nellie and I had two days here alone and a lovely gossip.' Their peace was interrupted by the arrival of a married couple who were friends of Jos. 'The husband,' wrote Trudie, 'looks unwholesome and talks clever and makes lewd and familiar remarks which make Nellie and me most proper and dignified.' One evening Nellie gave a dinner party.

'First we had a grandy tidy—gramophone records were arranged in a pile, old papers destroyed, cigarette tins emptied into a silver box and other garbage removed by its owners to their own quarters. The flowers were very fine, arranged in two silver goblets which looked most handsome when I had polished the silver with my toothpaste. After the tidy, I washed my hair and dressed in my green pyjamas, embroidered coat and my mosquito boots. Nellie wore black pyjamas and black and blue coat, and the dogs were banished for the evening.'

When two of the guests failed to turn up, it was decided to begin dinner without them. The soup had just been finished when

'the door opened and in came Mr Evelyn Waugh—but no Raymond de Trafford. With many apologies he explained that Mr de T. hadn't come home, and so Mr Waugh had hired a car from Nakuru 20 miles away and he and two black gentlemen had been wandering round the countryside looking for the house. Mr Waugh was dressed in a grey flannel suit and a crimson polo jumper with a high neck which did something to counterbalance the decolletage of the other men. Very soon after dinner all the lights went out and the candles were only long enough to see us to bed; all of which Nellie pointed out to the party and so sent them away. A very good evening which finished by about 10.30. This morning there was a sad voice at the telephone asking Nellie what time it was; this was Mr Waugh who said all the clocks had stopped, no sign of Raymond de Trafford's return, and worst of all no food in the house. Nellie sent a car for him and he came here and had breakfast and then went with us for a day in the country, a picnic and a fish in the Molo river.'

Plans had been made for a trip to Kilimanjaro, riding part of the way up the mountain, but the difficulty and expense of hiring ponies proved too great.

'I was enchanted,' wrote Trudie in her diary, 'I think seven would have been too many and I was rather alarmed at the idea of going through elephant country. I should hate to meet a couple of elephants crossing the road with probably no tree to climb and no way to get past them! So instead of Kilimanjaro, Nellie has arranged a nice safe trip to Uganda, just for Nellie, Judy, Mr Waugh and me. Mr Waugh was anxious to start fairly soon as he had been with Raymond de Trafford for some days and failed sometimes to get any breakfast, so Nellie suggested he should start by train a day earlier, visit priests and missionaries at Kisumu and be picked up by us there.'

On January 18th, Nellie, Trudie and Judy set off for Uganda.

'At 8 o'clock we stepped proudly into our borrowed Ford, all very smart in trousers or jodhpurs and Nellie in her long-shorts. These last garments are peculiar to Nellie and are the result of her passion for having her clothes washed each time she wears them. Except for her best jodhpurs, all her everyday bifurcated garments now end about halfway between her knee and ankle which gives her a very jaunty look. She maintains she is the exact replica of Gainsborough's "Boy with a Rabbit", and there certainly is some resemblance.

'The Ford refused to start but as our drive is 4 miles downhill, we started off undaunted. For 2 miles Nellie tried top gear and low gear and we turned every knob we could see but got no sign of a spark. We then stopped and Judy and Nellie had a lovely time undoing nuts and discussing what was the cause of the trouble. I sat in the sun, admiring the native children who had gathered round and wondering how one, about 6 years old, could look so contented with a fairly large baby on his back, supported by a strap round his forehead. I began to wonder when Judy's and Nellie's passion for mechanics would be satisfied and they would send for another car. This happened in about half an hour.' Kisumu on Lake Victoria was 120 miles away and the road descended 6,000 feet from the highlands, but they eventually got there about 3 o'clock, 'very hungry, but delighted to see Mr Waugh patiently waiting for us.' The party then pushed on to Soy to stay with friends, and got there at 9, 'Nellie having driven for 11½ hours and done 240 miles refused to admit she was the least tired!'

The next day they drove on into Uganda.

'Judy and Mr Waugh noticed many differences in topography and types of natives when they passed from Kenya to Uganda, and were much disappointed when they found they were about 20 miles out as to the position of the boundary.' They stopped for the night at Jinja, 'a nice place, and Lake Victoria an inland sea, impressive enough to make it right for the Nile to have chosen it as its source. Uganda not half as nice as Kenya, not such friendly smiling natives and too hot to be comfortable, but the roads very much better.'

From Jinja they made an expedition to Kampala and Entebbe.

'A good run there and back, only marred by the fact that we dropped Mr Waugh (by now pronounced Mr Wuff) at Kampala, and it seemed a sad spot in which to leave him for five days until he could get a boat and find his way to Liberia to study the only native republic.'

On their way back to Kenya, they decided to go by Kakamega and Eldoret to the Ridleys where they were to stay. The road was terrible, even by Kenya standards. Coming to a deep chasm, they found a framed notice on the bridge saying, 'This Bridge is unsafe.' So they turned back to Kakamega and presently met a European in a car. When Trudie asked him about the bridge, he answered, 'Oh, yes, we mended it this morning, but haven't yet taken the notice down!' Beyond the bridge the road deteriorated into a narrow track through a forest and they saw a notice reading, 'Road probably impassable owing to logging operations.' By this time there was only an hour of daylight left. However by luck and Nellie's skilful driving they got to Eldoret by eight o'clock, having met a leopard crossing the road just in front of them.

After a happy and restful day's fishing at the Ridleys', they came home to Njoro. 'The last week at Njoro was very pleasant,' Trudie wrote in her diary, 'Nellie and Judy had four days of polo which Judy adored. I watched one day, but didn't really like it.' Apart from calling on and dining with neighbours, 'Judy and I painted most of my bathroom and I oiled Nellie's Zanzibar chest which improved it greatly. I stained a piece of furniture, which the dogs had bitten, with permanganate of potash, which I thought was a very ingenious thing to think of and then found that it is well known as being a furniture stain.' On the way to Nairobi they stopped at Lake Elmenteita to see the flamingoes. 'When thousands of them rose from the water it was as though acres of peach blossom were being blown across the lake,' wrote Trudie.

Nellie Grant travelled back to England with Trudie and Judy. They had 'a wonderfully good voyage' home. This time Trudie refused to be on the Sports Committee and spent an idle and restful fortnight, reading and helping Nellie with her 'life's work'— a large piece of embroidery.

'I do petit point very slowly and rather badly,' Trudie wrote, 'and find it a most irritating occupation. At last I have read Priestley's "Good Companions" and thoroughly enjoyed the sentiment and the happy ending which never gave me a moments anxiety. I think it is most peculiar that people think that it is a good book in these sophisticated days.'

With the words, 'We have had an extraordinarily pleasant trip and the Fates have been very kind to us,' Trudie ended the diary of her Kenya interlude.

CHAPTER XII

The Land Army and the early War Years

(i)

On April 9th 1938 the Permanent Secretary of the Ministry of Agriculture called a meeting of four of his senior officials to discuss the question of farm labour in England and Wales in the event of war. Only one set of decisions was reached, but these were the important ones that arrangements should be proceeded with 'for setting up a Women's branch of the Ministry in time of war'; that 'Lady Denman should be invited to take charge of it'; and that, in consultation with Lady Denman, a list should be prepared of people suitable for one or two of the subordinate posts, and that Lady Denman should also be consulted about the functions of Women's County Committees and about the selection of their Chairmen.

Trudie's first reaction to the Ministry's approach was to consider its bearing on her responsibility as head of the Women's Institutes. In view of her Land Army experience in World War I, it seemed clearly her duty to accept, however reluctant she might personally be—and she was 54 and only recently recovered from a very grave illness—provided that her acceptance did not damage the Institutes. As to that, she knew that in Miss Hadow the Institutes had a most able and experienced deputy leader. Moreover the women most suitable for County leaders and organizers in a Land Army would have to be largely drawn from the ranks of the Institutes, so that Trudie's own dual position might well be of positive advantage. When she consulted the National Federation's Executive Committee, they at once agreed with these views and urged her not to give up the Federation's Chairmanship. It was, therefore, at the Institutes' headquarters in Eccleston Street that, as a top-secret operation, Trudie and Miss Farrer, the Federation's General Secretary, began to work out the detailed plans for a wartime Land Army. Using the Institutes' lists, Trudie was able from personal knowledge, to put down the names of those, who, in her opinion, would best fill the key posts; and on May 14th, she wrote, in confidence, to her chosen candidates for the Chairmanship of each County Committee.

Three days earlier, as Chairman of the Women's Institutes, Trudie had received a letter from the Home Secretary, telling her that he was setting up a body, based on the chief women's organizations, for enrolling volunteers for air-raid precautions. A Grand Council was to be formed under the name of the Women's Voluntary Services, with the Dowager Lady Reading as Chairman. The subject of the role of the Institutes in war had already been exercising the minds of Trudie and her Executive Committee. It was a difficult question, but they now came to the conclusion that if the Movement was to be true to its principle of non-sectarianism, it must, out of respect for the beliefs of its Quaker members, impose restrictions upon its participation, as a Movement, in war work, even though they realized that such refusal to disregard minority beliefs in a time of national crisis would arouse criticism both inside and outside the Institutes.

Trudie, accordingly, helped to draw up and signed a statement of policy which was issued to all Institutes in June (1938). The statement told the Institutes that the Executive considered that, in the event of war, the Institutes could give valuable help by arranging hospitality for evacuated mothers and children and by assisting, as good neighbours, in home safety services. But air-raid precaution work should not be undertaken by the Women's Institutes as an organization, since this responsibility lay with the local authorities and concerned men and women equally.

The Munich crisis of that autumn found the Government's evacuation scheme still incomplete and the Home Office asked the Institutes for immediate help if needed. But the crisis passed and, before long, the Government's scheme was ready, using the organization of the Women's Voluntary Services. The Institutes' own evacuation plans, which Trudie helped Miss Farrer to draw up, were thus never utilized, although, when war came, almost every Institute member became personally involved in the reception and care of the evacuees.

On the Land Army front, Trudie, after Munich, had asked her County Chairmen designate to form their Committees against possible emergencies. That autumn she was vainly urging the Minister of Agriculture to meet the Chairmen so as to retain their keenness and deter them from committing themselves to other work. As 1939 came in she grew increasingly worried at the Ministry's apparent lack of realism over war preparations, but it was not until March that her repeated requests obtained an interview with the Minister, Mr Dorman Smith. When she finally saw him she presented a memorandum urging that the shadow County Chairmen should be allowed to find out which farmers would be willing to take land girls and where billets could be found, and that a decision should be taken about minimum wages. Official cold water was, however, firmly poured on her proposals, the Treasury writing to the Ministry that Lady Denman's ideas were 'a sledge-hammer to crack a nut'. At the end of April, Trudie felt obliged to deliver an ultimatum that she would be forced to resign unless she was allowed to choose and appoint her headquarters staff. This produced the desired effect, the Permanent Secretary replying that he recognized that 'her request was completely reasonable'. Trudie promptly enlisted Mrs Jenkins, whose outstanding ability was well-known to her from the days when she had served as General Secretary of the Institutes' National Federation. She was given a temporary appointment as Trudie's 'personal assistant'.

From now on things began to move, the Ministry agreeing that preparations should be made on the lines of Trudie's memorandum. Local Education authorities and farmers were asked to be ready to train women in tractor driving and other skilled farm work, the County Committees were officially recognized and given paid secretaries and staffs, and a recruiting campaign for land girls was started. In June Trudie even obtained her London Conference of County Chairmen, the Permanent Secretary of the Ministry subsequently writing to her that in his long experience of conferences he had 'never seen business despatched so quickly and speeches so relevant and so short.' In February Trudie had put forward the proposal that, in the event of war, the Land Army should use her own house at Balcombe as its headquarters free of charge. At the end of July her offer was gratefully accepted.

In her speech at the Women's Institutes' Annual General Meeting that summer of 1939, Trudie explained to the delegates the Executive's general plans for the Movement should war come.

'We believe,' she said, 'that it is essential that Women's Institutes in their anxiety to help in a time of national crisis should not lose sight of their peacetime functions. They should continue to be centres of activity for the educational and social life of countrywomen, and their efforts to improve country life should not cease. At the same time it is obvious that Women's Institutes *can* give and are giving the most valuable help with regard to plans for the reception of city children in the villages. It is also obvious that if the great disaster of war should overtake us, the authorities will look to the Women's Institutes to give their help in increasing food production and in looking after members of the Women's Land Army in addition to caring for evacuated town dwellers.'

(ii)

The administrative headquarters of the new Women's Land Army was set up at Balcombe Place on August 29th, five days before war began. Under Trudie as Honorary Director, with Mrs Jenkins as Assistant Director, there were fourteen officers and thirty-five clerks and typists, mostly from the Ministry of Agriculture in London. The Ministry also insisted on the presence of one of its higher officials as Chief Administrative Officer to be responsible for finance and for correspondence with Government Departments and Local Authorities.

When the headquarters staff arrived at Balcombe station from London, they found all the Balcombe Place cars, including Trudie's Rolls-Royce, waiting to take them to their new home, where they were refreshed with cocktails while their bedrooms were being allocated. The whole of Balcombe Place had been re-arranged for its new use. Trudie had her own office in a business room off the big hall, which housed the clerical staff. Mrs Jenkins occupied the library, which became a social room for the senior staff in the evenings. The junior staff had the music room for their recreational use. All the staff slept by ones or twos in the lovely Balcombe bedrooms, except for one dormitory holding six of the youngest. The stables and squash court were given over to Uniform stores.

Never did staff enjoy pleasanter surroundings or a friendlier atmosphere for their work than in Trudie's home. One of the typists—a young widow from London—has described their life at Balcombe. In the lovely September weather that greeted their arrival and in subsequent summers the girls used to swim in the garden pool before breakfast and were free to wander at will about the grounds. Tennis and hockey were organized. Indoors there was a gramophone in the music room and dancing, table-tennis and darts. There were electric kettles for tea-making and parties in the bedrooms, and a laundry room for washing and ironing. The dining-room was arranged in small tables for six, with a high table for Trudie and the senior staff in the window embrasure. Trudie always took her meals with the staff and all shared the same food, which, though later severely handicapped by strictly-observed rationing, maintained a high standard in Mrs Missenden's capable hands. She even provided fresh scones for the staff's 'clevenses'. Trudie saw to it that her headquarters' atmosphere was informal. Except for punctuality at meals on which she insisted, there were no rules. Off duty, the staff could come and go as they liked, and if they came in late at night there were always biscuits and milk left out for them. They could pick all the flowers they wanted, but when they picked a bunch, Trudie asked them to pick another to give to the hospitals.

Even under such conditions there were, of course, grumblers. Trudie took special delight in the highly critical attitude of one cockney junior. When fresh fruit salad was served, this girl would remark 'No custard today', until Bird's custard powder was specially procured; and she was heard to complain, 'What, roast pheasant *again!*' But when Trudie organized a Christmas treat and went with all the staff in a coach to the cinema in Haywards

Heath, to return to an informal meal in the kitchen, it was this cockney girl who started the singing of 'For she's a jolly good fellow'.

When Trudie was not away attending conferences and rallies, she used to work in her office all the mornings and again in the late afternoons. After dinner she would take part with the staff in table-tennis, darts and other games. Her bed-time was half-past nine. Lord Denman gave up living at Balcombe ten days after the Land Army's arrival, moving to a hotel in Hove where he subsequently set up house. But he came over to Balcombe periodically on Sundays.

It was, of course, no easy task for Trudie to get her own domestic staff to continue to serve under the new conditions and to overcome their dislike for ministering to people whom they considered to be their 'inferiors'. That she was able to do so was a tribute to the love and loyalty she had inspired. 'That was a trying time for the staff,' the butler later remarked. 'And then those Whitehall people always trying to show her Ladyship that she didn't know how to run it.' It was even more trying for Trudie to give up her home to the Land Army. It meant no privacy except in her bedroom, no getting away from the atmosphere of work and worries, and only too frequently, being met, on her return tired out from some long wartime journey, by the need to exert all her tact to soothe ruffled feelings.

(iii)

The administration of the Women's Land Army involved special problems. The essential difference between the land girls and the women in the Services was that the latter were collectively employed by the State, enjoyed all the advantages of a community existence and were subject to Service discipline, while the former were, in most cases, individually employed by individual farmers and worked in obscure isolation. Dismissal by the employing farmer, or, ultimately, expulsion from the Land Army were the only disciplinary powers. With her belief in devolution, the organization which Trudie set up to meet the Land Army's need for individual care and treatment of its personnel was based on the Counties. Each County office had its honorary Chairman and Committee and its whole time salaried Secretariat. The County offices were responsible for interviewing recruits, enrolling them, arranging for their month's training and then placing them in their jobs. A third of the recruits came from London and the big industrial cities of the North, and were wholly ignorant of agricultural work. The County offices were also responsible for the land girls' subsequent welfare and conditions of employment. For liaison between her headquarters and the Counties Trudie engaged seven area organizers. In the Counties, each County office employed a small number of salaried organizers, but the personal link between the County headquarters and the individual land girl was mainly provided by local voluntary representatives. These representatives had to visit each land girl in their area once a month, seeing to her welfare and smoothing out her troubles, finding her a comfortable billet with often unwilling housewives, introducing her to neighbours and the local Women's Institute or Young Farmers' Club, and helping her to take advantage of the correspondence courses, proficiency tests and other Land Army activities. It was equally the representatives' duty to keep in close personal touch with the farmer, making sure that proper wages and overtime were being paid and off-time given, and firmly but tactfully dealing with difficult or unreasonable employers. The task of these voluntary representatives, so vital to the whole Land Army, was difficult and worrying. Yet they stuck to their jobs, even when later in the war they were experiencing so many restrictions in running their own homes.

It was a notable feat that Trudie was able to inspire and maintain the keenness and efficiency of an administration so largely composed of unpaid part-time workers. For one thing she never spared her efforts to keep personal touch with the Counties through frequent visits. For another, there was the clarity and simplicity of all the instructions she issued. Her County Chairmen were also made members of their County War Agricultural Committees, and they were struck by the contrast in the instructions they received in this capacity from the Ministry and the instructions they received on the same subject from Balcombe in their capacity as Land Army Chairmen. The former would cover three or four pages with involved bureaucratic language, the latter would follow the Churchillian directive of being expressed on one sheet in terms that the dullest could at once understand.

The administrative personnel in the Counties was very largely drawn from the Women's Institute movement. Trudie had herself picked the Chairmen, and many members of their staffs were personally known to her. Criticism from the Left arose from time to time about the composition of the County Committees and representatives on the grounds that they were too 'county' in the social sense. But Trudie considered that familiarity with country life and local conditions was more important than administrative experience, and that it was desirable that her County organization should largely be composed of women whom the farmers knew and respected and who were themselves familiar with all the problems of the employment of agricultural labour. Not all the County offices were run with equal efficiency, nor did all the amateur administrators prove capable of holding down their jobs, but the final justification for her policy and for the organization which she set up and inspired lay in the fact that in spite of the isolation of the land girls, the hard conditions of their work and their comparatively low pay, the wastage in a force which ultimately totalled 80,000 was surprisingly small and was actually less than the wastage among the highly paid women munition workers.

Throughout the war, Trudie's main problem with the Land Army was to regulate supply and demand. At first, her difficulty was to find employment for those who had volunteered and to keep those on the waiting list from seeking war work elsewhere. The farmers' initial prejudice against employing land girls had to be overcome through the good experience of those who made the experiment, through the increasing amount of work that farmers were called upon to undertake, and through the growing difficulty of obtaining male workers. It was the pioneer work of the 4,500 land girls for whom jobs had been found by the end of

December 1939 that convinced farmers that land girls were useful employees, and Trudie, in later speeches, would often refer to their efforts. The winter of 1939–40 was one of the hardest in living memory, but the girls—many of them town-bred and wholly unused to outdoor work—refused to be beaten by mud, snow and ice. Quickness and imagination often compensated for lack of physical strength, and the land girls played their full part in breaking to the plough the 2 million new acres that were ready for sowing in the spring of 1940. By April there were 6,000 land girls at work and Trudie was looking ahead to the need for extra labour for the 1940 harvest. For this, she proceeded to recruit an Auxiliary Force whose members could offer four weeks' seasonal service.

From the start the land girls suffered from being considered rather comic—a suitable butt for Press jokes and caricatures—while the glamour and prestige were given to the women in the Services. This, and neglect of the Land Army in Whitehall, hampered both recruitment and employment. Trudie had to fight an unremitting battle to try to secure better official and public recognition of the Land Army's value. A letter she sent to Mr Hudson, the new Minister of Agriculture, at the end of June (1940) shows some of the difficulties with which she was initially faced.

'I was most distressed,' she wrote, 'to hear Mr Hurd in his broadcast last night advise farmers wanting seasonal labour to apply either to the War Agricultural Committee or the Labour Exchange, and to hear no mention of the Women's Land Army. This will give farmers the impression that the Ministry does not consider the Land Army seriously as a source of labour, and it must add to the already loudly expressed dissatisfaction of the many volunteers whom the Land Army enrolled for seasonal work and who are now being told that they are not likely to be needed. Mr Hurd's omission is particularly unfortunate as, although I did not myself hear Mr Bevin's [the Minister of Labour] broadcast on Saturday, I am receiving protests that when discussing agricultural labour, he did not mention the Women's Land Army. These broadcasts will add to our troubles here. For the regular force we have recruited about 3,000 of the additional 5,000 volunteers we were told to enrol. Many of these are already in training, but as yet we have not got enough jobs for them. For the Auxiliary Force we have enrolled a very large number of volunteers on the estimate that these would be needed and that the need was urgent. Now, even the small demands which we have received for Auxiliary Force workers are being cancelled, partly because soldiers are being made available for farm labour at a very low rate. I shall be exceedingly grateful if you will help us by making very special reference to the W.L.A. when you broadcast to-morrow.'

Mr Hudson—who was always to do his best for the Land Army—complied with Trudie's request. In her letter of thanks she remarked, 'incidentally, from my personal point of view, it was a pleasure to hear the Land Army mentioned individually and not as one item of a mixed bag of conchies, prisoners of war, unemployed etc.!'

Whatever the neglect of the Land Army in most official circles, there was one source which never failed to give it invaluable support and encouragement. Both Queen Mary and Queen Elizabeth were Women's Institute members and knew and admired Trudie and her work. Already in March 1940, the Queen had arranged to attend a tea party at the Goldsmiths Hall to which the Goldsmiths Company invited 250 land girls drawn from every county in England and Wales. Trudie was commanded to come to Buckingham Palace to talk to the Queen beforehand, and she wrote to the Ministry's Public Relations Department that she hoped that the Queen's visit would 'counteract the unfortunate criticisms from which the Land Army suffered.'

Trudie felt that one method of promoting *esprit de corps* and a sense of unity among the widely-scattered individuals who made up her Army would be through the publication of their own monthly magazine. Fortunately she had at hand an ideal choice for editor in the person of her friend Margaret Pyke, who had been released from her Family Planning Association duties and had come to live at Balcombe when war broke out. The first number of *The Land Girl* came out in April 1940. It was initially an unofficial publication, though two years later it was officially sponsored by the Ministry, and it eventually enjoyed a circulation of 21,000. Each month Mrs Pyke contributed a wise and helpful leading article for the front page, and in her hands, the magazine, as well as giving much practical information, maintained a friendly and informal character. Trudie especially enjoyed the humorous touches which the magazine included, such as the would-be recruit who wrote that she wanted to learn to milk, but would like to begin on a calf; or the sad letter from the land girl who reported that she couldn't go to church because she had ploughed in her Land Army hat; or a girl's enthusiastic description of the T.T. dairy where everything was kept so wonderfully clean that they even scrubbed the milkmaids' seats twice a day; or the farmer who applied for a land girl capable of producing a few eggs and table chickens.

(iv)

Trudie now had, of course, less time to devote to the Women's Institutes. For the first few months of the war she was able, however, to rely on Miss Hadow, her Vice-Chairman. In October, Trudie issued a letter headed 'War Time Plans', which stated that the Institutes' first job, as requested by the Government, was to carry on their monthly meetings. The letter went on to emphasize the value of the Institutes' work in welcoming and helping to look after the welfare of evacuees and land girls, and then turned to the important part that the Government wished the Institutes to play in the production and preservation of the country's food through bigger supplies from gardens and allotments. 'Whatever adjustments we may have to make,' Trudie ended the letter, 'let us be sure that in all our work we continue the methods of self-government on which our movement is built.'

That December (1939) the National Federation, through the Institutes, organized a survey so as to give an accurate picture of the conditions of the evacuated mothers and children when they arrived in the villages. Only through the Institutes could such a survey have been undertaken, and when it was published in 1940 it had an important effect on current social thinking and on plans for post-war reconstruction. The survey described the widespread shock to the villages when they found that the habits of the evacuees were so startlingly less civilized than those that had long been accepted by countrywomen, who were horrified at the state of filth of many of the children and at finding women who could neither cook nor sew, but whose one idea was to visit the public-house or cinema. The introduction to the Survey ended by stating that the main desire of the Institutes was 'that steps should be taken without delay to tackle the weaknesses in our social system of which they have just had experience of such a distressing kind.'

In January (1940) the Movement sustained a wholly unexpected blow in the death of Miss Hadow. For Trudie, it meant the loss of a trusted personal friend, on whose wisdom and judgement she had relied through twenty years of the closest association. Although the National Federation was fortunate in the ability and character of the other war-time Vice-Chairmen, Miss Hadow's death threw a heavy extra burden on Trudie at a time when she could least afford it and when the Movement was losing many of its leading workers to the Services and other war activities, and was suffering, for the first time in its history, a decrease in membership.

In May, at the time of Dunkirk, Trudie was asked by the Government to broadcast to the Institutes. 'I have been lucky enough,' her talk began, 'to work with countrywomen for many years past, and I know their pluck, I know their resourcefulness, and I know their good sense. These great qualities are just what are wanted now.' She went on to speak of the need for their courage in the face of bad news, for their resourcefulness in helping with food supplies and in managing to give hospitality in their homes to children from the cities, and for their good sense in rejecting rumours and defeatist talk.

Later that summer she sent out another letter to the Institutes on the importance of their role in helping to safeguard the nation's food.

'I appeal,' she wrote, 'to those Committee members who, like myself, have undertaken other national work in addition to their Women's Institute work to do their utmost to see that the nation's food supply does not suffer owing to their dual responsibilities. I feel that food production and preservation is the work on which we country people must concentrate, and we must realize that other valuable efforts such as Red Cross working parties which do not depend mainly or only on country people must take second place.'

In any case Trudie's own responsibilities were both concerned with countrywomen and with food production.

Yet another commitment which Trudie felt obliged to undertake in the early months of 1940 was membership of the Rushcliffe Committee, which the Government had set up to help secure the best utilization of Voluntary Organizations in the war effort. Miss Hadow had been selected for membership, and, on her death, the Government asked Trudie to take her place. On paper, the Committee under Lord Rushcliffe's Chairmanship was a most impressive body. Fortunately for Trudie with all her other pre-occupations, it was soon found that, on their own initiative, the Voluntary Organizations had already successfully fitted themselves into their respective Governmental spheres. There was, therefore, little need for the Rushcliffe Committee's intervention and its work quietly petered out.

The war had largely brought the activities of the Family Planning Association to a standstill. Nearly all the staff were absorbed in other directions, and the headquarters' office was moved to Bournemouth, where the chief organizer carried on single-handed. Executive meetings at which Trudie always took the chair were, however, still held in London. She was also still attending London meetings of the Carnegie United Kingdom Trust; and, in her capacity as director of the Westminster Press, she continued to be harassed by the differences between the editors and Spender who never ceased to champion Chamberlain, and who wrote her frequent letters complaining that he was being cold-shouldered and his advice ignored at the Westminster Press monthly conferences. After consulting with her brother Clive, Trudie tried to compose these differences, but with little success. Her own faith in Spender's wisdom remained unshaken. She wrote to congratulate him on his optimistic articles in the *Sunday Times*, and, after Chamberlain's resignation, expressed to him her dismay at articles in Westminster Press newspapers which indulged in 'post-mortem criticism of the late Prime Minister'. In 1941, however, Spender wrote to her to say that the hatchet had been buried. Soon afterwards he died in harness.

CHAPTER XIII

The Land Army and the later War Years

(i)

In the spring of 1941, when the numbers of the Women's Land Army had reached 13,000, Trudie succeeded in freeing it from the direct control of the Ministry of Agriculture. It was agreed that while it would remain the responsibility of the Minister it would become a 'semi-independent Unit Organization'. This meant that Trudie, as its Honorary Director, was empowered to make all day-to-day administrative decisions, as well as appointments and promotions. She could also incur expenditure on uniforms, propaganda etc. within a fixed annual sum of money.

On achieving in 1941 this measure of independence Trudie wrote to Buckingham Palace to ask if there would be any chance of the Queen becoming the Land Army's Patron. Her Majesty at once accepted. Thereafter, their Patron's interest in the land girls was shown in many ways. Her portrait was sent for display in the head recruiting office in London, she sent special messages at Christmas and on other occasions, she made a point of reviewing land girls when on tours, and became the Patron and a generous subscriber to the Land Army's Benevolent Fund. In July 1943, a fourth birthday party for over 300 land girls was held at Buckingham Palace. It was characteristic of the Queen's thoughtfulness that although the day was fine she arranged for the party to be held indoors, rightly thinking that it would be the splendour of the big rooms and their furnishings that the girls would most like to see. In writing to thank her, Trudie said that she was charged with messages from the girls who never thought that the Queen would talk with them or that she would know all about the Land Army and their work. In fact, land girls were employed on all the royal estates. The personal interest shown by the Queen did much to dispel the feeling of neglect from which the Land Army suffered and greatly heartened Trudie in the constant battle which she had to fight with the authorities on behalf of her girls.

Better wages was one of the issues. In the autumn of 1940 Trudie was demanding a uniform minimum wage on the grounds that 'in the low-wage counties lodgings were often expensive and vice-versa.' A few months later the minimum wage was agreed in principle by the Ministry of Agriculture. She had to fight, too, for the agricultural novelty of a day off a week for the girls. Then there was a battle to obtain extra rations for the land girls as for other workers in heavy industry. This, too, was finally won. Trudie fought successfully, as well, over such matters as sick pay and holidays with pay. A further hard but eventually won battle was over the admission of land girls to service canteens. Uniforms and clothing were the source of yet another constant struggle. It seemed to Trudie to be most unfair that her girls, whose work exposed them to all weathers, should be less generously treated than women in the Air Raid Precaution services in parts of the country where air aids were virtually unknown. Nor was she satisfied with the cut of the Land Army's short overcoat. Consultations with her own tailor led to the girls' coat being the best cut of all those worn in the Women's Services. The administrative staffs in many of the counties felt that, as was the case in the Women's Voluntary Services, they should also wear uniform. This view was not shared by all the counties, nor by Trudie. In forwarding the request to the proper quarter (who turned it down) she prefaced her letter by remarking that she was far too old to enjoy wearing a uniform herself. Trudie also fought hard for awards for courage shown by land girls. There had been many cases in the east and south coast counties of girls carrying on with their jobs under enemy air attack, and, in Kent, even under enemy gunfire from across the Channel. Eventually, in 1942, some awards were given.

But Trudie's sternest fight was with Mr Ernest Bevin and his Ministry of Labour. Not unnaturally, perhaps, the Ministry resented the 'semi-independent' status of the Land Army, whose County Committees conducted their own recruiting instead of working through the Ministry's Employment Exchanges, whose personnel was outside the control of the Ministry's Essential Works Order, and whose inspection was carried out by its own staff instead of by the Ministry's Welfare Department. Trudie was, however, determined to keep her organization as free as possible from bureaucratic control, and with the help of Mr Hudson, the Minister of Agriculture, she succeeded.

Meantime, the Women's Land Army was steadily expanding to meet the ever growing demand from the farmers who, through good experience, had forgotten their former prejudices and were eagerly asking for more land girls. In June 1940, on the Land Army's first birthday, there had been 7,000 employed volunteers. In June 1941 the number had risen to 14,000. In June 1942 the strength was 40,000 and in June 1943 65,000. Before the end of 1943 the total reached 80,000, but, although the demand for 100,000 existed, the War Cabinet then decided that recruiting must be stopped because of the needs of other industries for women's labour. In the First World War, the maximum number in the Land Army had been only 23,000.

When the County War Agricultural Committees became direct employers of labour for special work such as land reclamation and threshing, they employed many land girls, working in gangs and living in hostels whose equipping, servicing and inspection gave Trudie and her Balcombe headquarters an additional responsibility. A Timber Corps was also started in 1942, and the next year there were over 4,000 land girls employed in forestry. It was also in 1942 that Trudie started and became Chairman of the Land Army's Benevolent Fund, which took extra care of cases of illness and disability, gave compassionate grants to girls out of work and helped with training and educational grants and with loan capital. The fund still continues its good work. At the end of April 1944, the headquarters staff were moved back to London. But as soon as the 'doodlebugs' started later that year, Trudie was asked to reopen Balcombe for the headquarters offices. They remained there until the war was over.

All through these war years Trudie was touring the country from Northumberland to Cornwall and from Norfolk to Wales, visiting county headquarters and attending conferences and rallies. Her conscience would not allow her to use a large comfortable car. Instead, so as to save petrol, Burnett drove her in her secretary's little Austin. But her strength was sapped by the long drives in a small car, through all weathers, poring over the map to find the way over roads without signposts, at night with only the dim blacked-out headlamps to lighten the darkness. At the end of the journey, there would only be cold war-time austerity to greet her in house or hotel. She was also involved in constant personal negotiations and conferences in London with Ministers and Government Departments. In London, too, she held regular conferences with her County leaders, when her skill as a Chairman reduced intricate official questions to clear and simple terms, and where all who attended were given full opportunity to ventilate their own special problems.

Then there were many recruiting broadcasts, all of which demanded careful and anxious preparation, and a broadcast to Australia on the occasion of the first birthday of the Australian Land Army. In 1943, when the Land Army at home was reaching its peak in numbers, Trudie was already looking forward to the return of peace in the hope that the bridge built by the war between town and country would not be broken down.

'I don't want all this to end with the war,' she said in a broadcast. 'I want all those of you who return to towns to keep with you always your understanding of the life and problems of the country, of the need for the kind of houses and education in the country which will give its dwellers and its children as good an opportunity as the towndwellers and children get. And I want those of you who stay in the country to take your part in the fight for the conditions which are essential to a good life.'

(ii)

In October 1940, the Women's Institute headquarters had been forced to leave London, and the National Federation's monthly Executive meetings were held in Oxford. In spite of all the demands made on her by the Land Army, Trudie regularly presided at them and never relaxed her direction of the Institutes' war-time policy. Her visits to Oxford were the occasion of a passage of arms with officialdom when she was refused petrol coupons for her very small car for her journeys from Balcombe. Trudie took the matter up direct with Lord Woolton.

'I cannot remain Chairman of the Women's Institutes,' she wrote to him, 'unless I can attend meetings. If I have to resign because I can't get petrol, the Institutes will draw the conclusion that the Government does not place any value on their national work, and this will certainly have a very discouraging effect on their efforts. A statement that the shortage of petrol is such that none can be spared to enable me to carry out my Institute work will not, I think, carry conviction as Institute members are well aware of the allowances made to other organizations and individuals.'

Needless to say the coupons she needed were quickly forthcoming.

War conditions prevented the Institutes from holding their Annual General Meetings except in 1943, when the delegates again came to the Albert Hall in London. Trudie, as usual, presided. In her speech she began by describing what the Institutes had done to further the national war effort.

'The special help given by the Institutes,' she said, 'has been great and varied. They responded nobly to the call for homes for evacuated children. They have given their services willingly to the preservation scheme whereby some 3,000 tons of fruit and vegetables have been saved. Through the Produce Guild and Institute Markets they have helped to grow more fruit and vegetables and to arrange for their distribution. They have in many counties forwarded the provision of school meals and the distribution of special food for children. Institutes have helped considerably to spread the knowledge of their crafts and to organize "make and mend" displays and classes. There is no doubt that to our dying day the words—salvage—war savings —herbs—hips and haws and meat pies will bring back poignant memories to all of us, but they will also remind us of practical work well done. I must also say a word of personal thanks for the hospitality extended to the Land Army and emphasize the enormous help you can give by offering to billet and look after volunteers in your homes. I cannot refer to everything that Institutes have done, but perhaps their greatest achievement is that, despite claims and difficulties, they have kept up their monthly meetings, their social half hours, their acting and singing. Through these and above all through their spirit of comradeship, they have helped to keep up the courage of the country population in times when courage has been badly needed. It is said that democratic organization is a handicap in the stress of war, but our work has been done through the ordinary machinery of the Institutes and by elected Committees, the County and National Federations and their elected representatives, and it cannot, I think, be said that Institutes have failed.'

Trudie went on to speak of the future. As early as 1941, she had addressed the Institutes' Consultative Council on the need for planning for post-war reconstruction, and that year the National Federation had submitted to the Government a memorandum outlining the Institutes' suggestions for the future of the countryside. Now she congratulated the Annual General Meeting on the sound beginning that the Institutes had made towards carrying out their post-war responsibilities—the promotion of international understanding as the foundation on which the future of the world must be built—the consideration and active presentation of the needs of countrywomen in education, health and housing—the taking by women of a larger share in local government.

'When you go home tomorrow,' she ended her speech, 'will you make it your business to find out how many women are serving on your Parish, District and County Councils? And will you do your best to get really practical and intelligent women to stand for election to these bodies? It is clear to me that we have not always exercised to the full our great democratic responsibility for putting forward our best people to be our leaders. My final word is don't forget that the young people coming home after the war will be our leaders of the future.'

Four thousand Institutes answered a questionnaire on general education, and were congratulated by the authorities on the practical way in which the evidence was collected and presented. Three thousand five hundred Institutes also replied to a questionnaire on the subject of piped water supplies and drainage in the villages. The results, published as a pamphlet in 1944, gave a vivid picture of the hardship and squalor caused by the general lack of these facilities. This was one of Trudie's favourite causes, and she personally sent copies of the pamphlet to six Cabinet Ministers and to a long list of other influential people. The framing of the Rural Water Supplies and Sewage Act of 1944 and the Water Act of 1945 owed much to the evidence which the Institutes had collected.

Trudie was herself directly involved in post-war reconstruction problems as a member of the Scott Committee. This important Committee was set up by the Government in the autumn of 1941 under the Chairmanship of Lord Justice Scott to advise on building, other constructional development, and the location of industry in country areas, having regard to the well-being of rural communities and the preservation of rural amenities. There had been some difficulty in securing Women's Institute representation on the Committee, and the National Federation insisted on Trudie representing them, hard as it was for her to spare the time. She felt sure, however, of a welcome from Lord Justice Scott as he had been Chairman of the Agricultural Organization Society when the Women's Institutes were under its aegis. The Committee began its work in October 1941 and continued to sit until the end of July 1942, holding sixty meetings and examining a host of witnesses. It is easy to see Trudie's hand in many of the recommendations of the Majority Report which she signed. Amongst other things, it stressed the importance of good rural housing, the need for women to serve on local authorities, for making electricity available throughout the country at no higher prices than that paid by the urban consumer, for the provision of rural water supplies, of village halls and playing fields—all matters on which the Institutes had campaigned for many years. The Report recommended the establishment of a Central Planning Authority to advise Government Departments and local planning authorities. Amongst the proposals for preserving the amenities of the countryside as well as securing access and enjoyment by town-dwellers, was the recommendation for the establishment of National Parks and Nature Reserves. Much, indeed, of what has since been done for the countryside can be found in the Scott Report's recommendations, in whose framing the detailed knowledge of country conditions provided by Trudie and the Institutes was a powerful influence.

One worrying responsibility which pursued Trudie in the midst of her other war-time pre-occupations was her Chairmanship of the Cowdray Club. Membership went down with the war and it became an increasing struggle to carry on in order that the Club's services should be available to nurses and professional women after the war. Fortunately, perhaps, there was much less to engage Trudie on the Family Planning front, although it was clear that public interest in the subject had not lapsed when a Sunday newspaper published a small paragraph saying that a leaflet, price 3d., was available from the Family Planning Association, and over 5,000 requests for the leaflet came in. Most of the clinics managed to keep open and from time to time Committees met at Eccleston Square. The Association's Annual General Meeting was also revived in 1943, when Trudie took the chair, as she did at a branch conference held the same year. A sub-fertility Committee was also set up, and, the year after, a Seminological Centre was established in London. Trudie was also concerned with general questions of sex-education and, in 1943, was consulted by the Ministry of Health over the wording of pamphlets which they proposed to issue. Her reply was characteristic.

'I think,' she wrote, 'that the wording of all explanations to the young of the facts of sex should be simple, detached and very precise and should avoid the slightest sentimental or emotional suggestion. . . . No doubt the author of this pamphlet has made a gallant attempt, but I think that he has introduced an unfortunately sentimental note, e.g. "nine *whole* months", "a *little* baby". Also he has made what the other and better pamphlet calls "the act of mating" appear such a fortuitous affair that I fear it will give as misleading an impression to the young, as it does a humorous one to their elders.'

(iii)

As early in the war as the spring of 1942, an official of the Ministry of Agriculture had written to Trudie to tell her that he had been unable to convince the interdepartmental Committee on the 'Further Education of Demobilized Members of H.M. Forces and Civil Defence Services' that the Land Army personnel should be included in any scheme that might be adopted. Trudie at once replied that she found it 'strange that any Committee could think it reasonable that a civilian nurse should be eligible for training as a veterinary surgeon but that a member of the Women's Land Army should be debarred from this advantage.'

It was, of course, only one aspect of the long battle that Trudie was fighting for proper official recognition of the Land Army and its work. The land girls' devoted if unspectacular efforts for their country were certainly fully as hard and fully as valuable as those of women in Civil Defence and other auxiliary services, and it was as unthinkable to Trudie as it was repugnant to her sense of justice that the land girls should receive less generous treatment at the nation's hands. Nevertheless, it began to grow increasingly apparent that hers was not the view taken in high official circles. At the beginning of 1944, she learned that the Minister of Agriculture had failed to persuade the War Cabinet that the Land Army should be included in the 'Reinstatement in Civil Employment Act'. Trudie could only make a vain plea that consideration should be given to any girl who had volunteered for the Land Army and whose place in civilian employment was taken by another girl who subsequently entered some other Women's Service. 'It would seem most unfair,' she wrote, 'that the second girl should be held to have a prior claim for re-instatement.' She also tried to stake a claim for her land girls over clothing coupons and grants when they were demobilized. By the autumn of 1944, it was clear that Mr Hudson, the Minister of

Agriculture, had lost the fight and that the War Cabinet had definitely decided to exclude the Land Army from all the post-war benefits and privileges to be accorded to other Women's Services. Yet, as Trudie pointed out to Mr Hudson, the Government still wanted the Land Army to be maintained at full strength so as to meet the need for agricultural labour in the immediate post-war years.

Trudie made up her mind that her resignation was the only weapon left to her. At the worst, it would establish the principles for which she was fighting. At the best, its threat and, if necessary its subsequent implementation, might help to secure for the land girls some of the benefits now denied them. She wrote accordingly to Mr Hudson in November 1944 to say that her position would be impossible unless the Government changed its mind.

Trudie's health was now giving her family much anxiety. The long strain was proving too much. That winter gall bladder trouble became serious and the doctors advised an immediate operation. But she was determined that her health should not appear to be a reason for her resignation. Her illness was kept as quiet as possible and she refused to have the operation so long as there was anything she could still do to fight the land girls' battle.

Early in January (1945) the Permanent Head of the Ministry of Agriculture informed her that the Government's decision was final. But Trudie still waited until some announcement should be made in Parliament. It came on February 15th, when Mr Bevin stated that Resettlement Grants of up to £150 would be extended to Civil Defence and other auxiliary workers but not to the Women's Land Army. When pressed by questions, he could only say that the Land Army would be dealt with by the Minister of Agriculture, who, as Trudie knew, had been given no authority to do anything.

That evening she handed in her letter of resignation to Mr Hudson. She released it to the Press next day. As she told the reporters, she had accepted, albeit regretfully, the policy that post-war benefits should only be given to men and women in the Forces, but 'it was the last straw' when it was announced that these benefits were to be extended to Civil Defence Workers, while the Land Army was to be excluded.

Her letter to Mr Hudson ran as follows:

'I write with regret to notify you of the decision foreshadowed in my letter of November 23rd and to tender you my resignation from the Office of Honorary Director of the Women's Land Army for England and Wales.

'The Land Army is a uniformed service recruited on a national basis by a Government Department and the work which its members have undertaken, often at considerable financial sacrifice, is in my view as arduous and exacting as any branch of women's war work and of as great importance to this country. Yet they have been refused post-war benefits and privileges accorded to such other uniformed and nationally organized services as the W.R.N.S., the A.T.S., the W.A.A.F., the Civil Nursing Reserve, the Police Auxiliaries and the Civil Defence Services.

'The position is a serious one for Land Army members who will have as great need as those in other services of Government assistance in the problems of re-settlement. As you know, I have protested against the omission of the Land Army from various Government schemes and also against the decision, now announced, that capital grants to assist in re-starting business enterprises will be available after the war to men and women who have served whole time in the Forces, the Merchant Navy or the Civil Defence Services but not to members of the Women's Land Army. It is this latest decision which has led me to feel that I must resign my present appointment and that I can no longer appear to be responsible for a policy with which I do not concur.

'May I express to you my great regret at severing my connection with the Women's Land Army and my appreciation of the kindness and courtesy I have received from you and your Department.

'I cannot tell you how grateful I am for the co-operation I have received (often under difficult circumstances) from the Chairmen, Committees, County Secretaries and their staffs and from all those connected with the organization. I am extremely sorry not to be able to continue to work with the

Counties for the Land Army until the time comes for it to be disbanded. I have reached the decision to resign only because I have held the view that one of my chief functions has been to get a square deal for members of the Land Army and I have felt personal responsibility for policy affecting their welfare. The latest decision of the Government therefore made me decide that my position had become untenable.'

Her resignation, as Trudie had hoped, at once focussed public attention on the issue. Newspaper comment was most favourable to the Land Army's case, and when, a few days later, Mr Hudson was forced to state in Parliament that he was unable to give any information as to the Land Army's treatment, *The Times* in a leading article, after noting that the House of Commons was 'properly zealous in the desire to see land girls treated with the generosity which their invaluable service has merited', voiced general public opinion by saying that 'no fine distinctions must be allowed to debar the members of the Women's Land Army from their due reward on demobilization.' In Parliament, Mr Hudson paid a full tribute to 'Lady Denman's leadership and loyal service', and wrote to her that 'your resignation means a heavy loss. . . . Everyone knows the great success which has been achieved, but perhaps I and my Department alone are fully able to appreciate the skill with which you have dealt with many problems and the understanding and loyalty you have shown in carrying through policies under what have often been difficult conditions.'

Balcombe, meantime, was flooded with letters from land girls and their parents, from County Committees, from individual farmers and from National Farmers' Union branches, all supporting Trudie's stand, while offers of backing came from women's organizations and from the Liberal Party, Lady Violet Bonham Carter writing to Trudie to say that 'you will see that the Party is standing solidly behind you.' As soon as the resignation was published, the Queen sent a kind telephone message through her Lady in Waiting, which was followed by a letter saying that 'the Queen will do anything she can to help.'

Typical of the letters from land girls was the one which read,

'I joined in June 1939. I have lost my pre-war office job (they sacked me when I volunteered) and as far as the Government is concerned my future would be completely blank—my sole souvenir of five and a half years' loyal service a rather battered scarlet armlet—not even a discharge badge.' Miss Sackville-West, whose excellent book on the Land Army had been of great service to its morale, wrote that 'every land girl I have spoken to in the last four days has been enthusiastic in her appreciation—she [Lady Denman] really does care what happens to us.'

Many of the County Chairmen also wished to resign, but when they met in London a letter from Trudie was read urging them against such a course.

'My resignation,' she wrote, 'has I think drawn attention to the Government's ungenerous attitude to the Land Army and, much as I regret having had to take this action, the smooth running of the organization has not been impaired thereby, but the resignation of any officers in the counties or of others at headquarters would strike at the foundation on which the Land Army organization is built.'

That Trudie's resignation was producing some effect was evident when a deputation from the County Chairmen received a reply from the Minister that 'he was not unhopeful that some method would be found of giving tangible recognition to the Land Army.' Things were moving, too, in Parliament. Further questions were asked in the Commons on March 8th, but in his statement on War Gratuities, the Prime Minister laid it down that the benefits could not be extended to the Land Army without opening the door to unending claims from other classes of industry who received industrial or professional rates of pay. Trudie promptly replied in a circular giving the Land Army's case. In it, she pointed out that Mr Churchill's argument did not hold water since the land girls' rate of pay had consistently been far less than that of industrial women workers and was even 8s. 6d. a week less than that of women Civil Defence workers who were eligible for the benefits. In any case, the land girls differed completely from industrial workers in being members of an officially designated 'Army', in being clothed in a state-supplied uniform and in being pledged to mobile service.

A month later the issue was again raised in the Commons. One hundred and thirty-five members had put their names to a question to the Prime Minister to ask whether he had considered further representations about the Women's Land Army. But Mr Churchill was again adamant in his refusal to modify the position taken up by the Government that the Land Army's case fell into the general industrial sphere.

Nevertheless the pressure being brought on the Government, coupled with the difficulty of getting badly needed recruits for the Land Army, led to something being done. On May 16th, Mr Hudson was able to announce in Parliament that concessions were being made whereby Land Army members would receive state help in training for agriculture or for other work in a comparative degree to the help to be afforded to Civil Defence and Auxiliary war workers. The Government also promised a grant of £150,000 to the Land Army's Benevolent Fund, and, on demobilization, the girls would be allowed to retain their greatcoats, if dyed navy blue, and their shoes. In spite of bitter protests from Members of Parliament that these concessions were 'mean and niggardly' and 'most disappointing and totally inadequate', the Government would do no more.

At the end of March, when she had finished briefing Members of Parliament, Trudie had her operation. It was successfully performed and, the day after, she was reading the newspapers.

The Land Army headquarters continued at Balcombe under Mrs Jenkins for the time being. In 1948, the County Committees were dissolved. The Land Army itself was wound up at the end of 1950. A final parade was held at Buckingham Palace. The Queen invited Trudie to come and watch it from inside the Palace, but, at the time, she was not well enough to accept. In her farewell message, the Queen said,

> 'The Land Army will not in any case be only an affectionate memory, since it will live still in the shape of thousands who have settled down in the countryside as the wives of farmers and farm workers, or who are themselves continuing to work

in agriculture when the organization itself comes to an end—in field and forest, garden, orchard and dairy.'

The Women's Land Army had, indeed, done more than recruit and organize 80,000 girls to help grow more food to meet the nation's desperate need, outstandingly successful as this had been. It had broken down farmers' prejudices, never to return; it had brought fresh blood and fresh ideas into the countryside; it had won for women a permanent place in British agriculture.

Trudie could justly be proud of her achievement. Without her driving power, without her determination to get attention paid to the Land Army's needs, without the confidence inspired by her disinterestedness and integrity, the Land Army's immense success would never have been achieved. Even though she had lost the final battle to obtain for her girls the rewards which she so deeply felt were their due, it may have been some consolation for her to know that her feelings were so widely shared. Notwithstanding her resignation she was given in 1951 the exceptionally high award of the Grand Cross of the British Empire. When the King invested her, he said, 'We always thought that the land girls were not well treated.'

CHAPTER XIV

The Last Years

(i)

In June 1945 the Women's Institute delegates once again assembled in the Albert Hall for their Annual General Meeting. Already the tide was turning and the war losses in membership were being made up. That year nearly 200 new Institutes were started, and membership increased by over 12,000. In the autumn the 6,000th Institute was formed, and the expansion proceeded so fast that, by the end of 1951, there were 7,700 Institutes with a total membership of close on 500,000. Such a post-war increase of more than 2,000 Institutes and 150,000 members over the pre-war peak was the best answer to the critics of Trudie's war-time policy and to those who thought that the Institutes might have lost their purpose.

In her Chairman's speech Trudie looked back with satisfaction on the part the Institutes had played in the war. 'There has hardly been a Government Department,' she said, 'which has not asked through our organization for the help and co-operation of countrywomen.' She also told of her encouragement in finding that so many more Women's Institute members were now serving on local government bodies, while the surveys that the Institutes had undertaken were strongly influencing official plans for rural improvements. She ended her speech by saying that although there might be fourteen townsmen to every countryman, 'let us have no false modesty in this matter of size and numbers. We can take heart by remembering that David was a country boy who did not let Goliath's size discourage him.'

The first full peace-time Annual General Meeting took place in May 1946. The Albert Hall was packed with the delegates, who made up a one hundred per cent representation of the Institutes linked in pairs, and with over 2,000 visitors. The Queen,

Aldeburgh Captain's Prize Competition, 1947
Left to right: Joy Winn, Trudie, Margaret Pyke, Lady Eddis

On the sands at Thorpeness with her granddaughter, Penelope, 1935

who was President of the Sandringham Institute, came to the
first day's meeting. Broadcasting to the Commonwealth a week
later Trudie described how, as Her Majesty arrived, 'a fanfare
was played by the trumpeters of the Household Cavalry, then
6,000 women from villages in England and Wales rose to their
feet cheering and waving, and when Her Majesty reached the
platform, we sang first "God Save the King", and then "Jerusalem".'

In her speech, the Queen said,

'I would like to take this opportunity, at this first peace-time
Annual General Meeting, of paying a tribute to Lady Denman
and congratulating her on all that the Women's Institutes have
accomplished under her leadership in peace and war. Lady
Denman has always steered with vision and has kept the
Women's Institutes' aims and ideals on a high level. She has led
with a just sense of proportion and balance, with the humour
which is so essential in a Chairman, and she has the quality
which a leader must have, that of being able to go on learning
and keeping up with the changing times. I suppose that Lady
Denman's contribution towards the happiness and progress
of rural life is one of the greatest that has been made in our time.
I hope she realizes the deep gratitude and affection which
members feel for her.'

It must be a rare event for Royalty thus to single out a living
individual for such a public tribute. It was, however, an exceptional occasion, since Trudie—although it was not yet known to
the Institutes—had told the Executive Committee that she would
not be a candidate for the Chairmanship at the next day's election.
She had always realized the danger of the Institutes falling too
much into the hands of their older members, and had always
encouraged bringing young blood into the leadership. After
nearly thirty years as Chairman, she felt that it was time that she
herself should firmly set the example. Earlier suggestions on her
part had met with the strongest protests from the Executive, but
now her resolve was strengthened by the knowledge that she had
found the right successor in Lady Albemarle, whose young, gay
and attractive personality was accompanied by the clear mind, the

firm grasp of essentials, and the practical wisdom and administrative ability on which Trudie set such store.

Trudie devoted most of her last speech as Chairman to the public issues on which she felt the Institutes should concentrate, reminding her audience of what their united efforts could do to bring about social reforms. As an illustration she told how it had been through the initiative of the Institutes and the pressure they had brought to bear that official regulations had been altered and the benefits of analgesia made available to country mothers. She also spoke of the need for encouraging young women to take up domestic work as a profession, since without domestic workers many reforms such as more maternity homes and more hospitals could not be achieved. 'Incidentally,' she added, 'if every woman, however unsuitable and unskilled, has to manage her home unaided, the public work of the country will have to be done entirely by men.'

She ended by speaking of the future.

'Planning is the order of our age,' she said, 'and some planners believe that the ordinary small village has no future and that people can only be happy if they live in a community of two or three thousand. Some of us, on the other hand, believe that a village with a few hundred inhabitants is a good place to live in—provided, of course, that water and electricity, which farms must have, go to the villages as well, and that the children can get to a good school. . . . I believe that this is the moment for country people to consider the problem from every point of view, the needs of agriculture, the employment likely to be available in the future, the demands of the cities, the advantages and disadvantages of living in a small community—and then to make their views known to all the planners, in the District, in the County, in the Region and in the National Government. For, after all, we country people have experience behind us; we have enjoyed a great heritage; and we must do our share in ensuring that in years to come the value and the delight of the country are not lost to our successors.'

Trudie's final words were to bear fruit when, two years later, a comprehensive questionnaire, covering all important rural amenities, was sent to the Institutes. The replies from nearly 7,000 villages were collated and published in a pamphlet entitled *Your Village*, which was very widely used and quoted.

The second day of the Annual General Meeting started with speeches from Miss Ellen Wilkinson, the Minister of Education, and from Lady Megan Lloyd George. Just before the luncheon interval, Miss Tennant, one of the Vice-Chairmen, asked the meeting to defer their discussion of a resolution. She had, she said, to make an announcement and it was

'one of the most difficult things I have ever done in my life, because I am here to tell you some news you are going deeply to regret and because words are a totally inadequate medium for what I am going to say. Lady Denman has decided not to stand for re-election as Chairman of the National Federation. I can hear your dismay and your bewilderment.' As one delegate reported, 'a tremendous sigh of consternation and regret filled the Albert Hall.' 'Two things I must say,' Miss Tennant went on. 'First, that although she would wish the success of the Movement to be attributed to the work of the members as a whole—and in that she is right—yet I am certain that it would never have acquired the character it has without her. . . . Secondly I must say something about her influence as Chairman of the National Executive Committee. She has not always suffered us gladly if we were very foolish, but her criticism has been of the kind that not only left no sting, but spurred us on to do better; and no one has been more generous with praise where praise was due. We who have been privileged to work with her will never be able to tell her how much we have learned from her.' Miss Tennant told the audience that Lady Denman had particularly asked that there should be no presentation to her. There was only one way Miss Tennant said 'by which we could show our gratitude and affection and that would be by each one of us resolving that the Movement, of which we are all so proud, shall go from strength to strength along the ways in which for 29 years she has so faithfully and wisely led us.'

A tremendous ovation greeted Trudie when she rose to reply.

'I should like you to know,' she said, 'that I think I have had an absolutely perfect job being your Chairman, because I think that countrywomen are the salt of the earth. I do not think they get a fair deal, and I have always thought that if we got together we could do something about it; and it has been extraordinarily satisfactory to me because we *have* been able to do something about it. It has given me the very greatest happiness. In fact I cannot tell you what a joy the work has been. I should like to tell you that another reason why it is such a nice job is that working with Institute members is good fun. They like jokes. They have not got an axe to grind, and do not show signs of personal ambition.'

Trudie went on to say that she had often tried to get someone else to stand for Chairman, but had always failed. Now she was taking the law into her own hands. The Institute Movement ought to have new and younger people—and she was 61. She was grateful for the suggestion that she should be given some kind of special office, but, while she would like to remain on the Executive Committee, she felt that the new Chairman should have the full responsibility and 'not have a President or anything of that kind floating about.'

A year before, it had been resolved that a Women's Institute College should be founded. Now, at the end of the meeting, Lady Albemarle rose to say,

'All this afternoon suggestions have been coming in of ways in which we can keep Lady Denman's name in perpetual association with the work of the Women's Institutes. . . . The most popular one is that the Women's Institute College should be known as the Denman College. We want this to be a memorial of the sort that would appeal to her.'

From the Chair, Trudie at once replied, 'I think that is a lovely idea. Thank you very much indeed,' and the Annual General Meeting closed.

From all over the country, Institutes and individual members wrote to Trudie in moving terms to express their gratitude to her and their sorrow at her giving up the Chairmanship. 'We have always felt so *safe* under your leadership,' ran a letter from Norfolk. 'We had somehow regarded you as being so permanent,' was the feeling of a Buckinghamshire Institute; and as a Gloucestershire Institute wrote, 'Lady Denman *is* the Institutes. We can't think of them apart from her.' A Cumberland Institute thought that 'Lady Denman has been the Movement's inspiration throughout'; and from Kent came the message that 'it must be a pleasant thing to know that in every village in England and Wales you will always be thought of with affection.' A letter from Lady Albemarle expressed the feelings of her successor.

'First of all,' she wrote, 'unconsciously you are a most wonderful instructor. One learns not only by observing your methods, but by your complete openness and honesty when you are yourself exploring a decision. When you do make a decision you have the courage not to waver and are not unduly moved by personal reactions. . . . Secondly your attitude to the newer members is one not of criticism but of exploration. This seems from my experience rather rare.'

Perhaps the Queen summed up the general feeling best when her Lady-in-Waiting wrote from Buckingham Palace that 'Her Majesty felt it a wonderful inspiration to see the affection with which our fellow-members regard you. I am to add, no wonder.'

(ii)

Towards the end of 1946, when she was just 62, Trudie developed the rheumatoid arthritis that was progressively to get more painful, although temporary relief was later given by Cortizone, then only obtainable with much difficulty. After the disease set in, she never fully recovered her spirits and zest. Physically, she had no wish to find substitute occupations more suited to failing health; and, mentally, it was depressing to face the fact that her powers were not as lively as they had been. In spite of her arthritis, she insisted in 1947 in taking part at Aldeburgh in the knock-out handicap competition for the Captain's ladies' golf prize. The competition involved playing two matches a day, and the field included players of international and national standard. Having won her earlier matches, Trudie faced her friend Joy Winn, the international player, in the semi-final on the morning of the last day. Trudie won on the 20th green, and went on, after lunch, to play Lady Eddis in the final. Her opponent was a player of national championship level and a local favourite, but the crowd, admiring Trudie's courage, were with the under-dog. Trudie won the match and the competition at the 17th hole. It was her last and greatest sporting triumph.

With the onset of ill-health Trudie began to shed some of her responsibilities. After the war she had continued to attend meetings of the Carnegie United Kingdom Trust in Scotland and in London, but, in 1948, she found that it was too much for her and resigned her place on the Executive Committee in favour of Lady Albemarle.

As a Director of the Westminster Press she had played an active part, with her brother Clive, in making post-war arrangements for the better guidance of the editorial policies of the group by the Directors with the help of outside experts. While she still firmly adhered to her Liberal principles, she found it difficult to decide whether support should be given to the Liberal Party. Posing this question to her brother, she asked whether the existence of the Liberal Party would provide a haven for the more intelligent Tories, or would it merely weaken the Tories and let in Labour? In fact, in 1945, she subscribed to the Liberal Party funds, but two years later she decided that it was unwise to commit the Westminster Press or herself to the direct support of a political party. At the end of 1949 she felt obliged, for health reasons, to resign her directorship, leaving the Board at a time when the papers were flourishing and enjoying record circulations. Three years later she resigned from her local Liberal Association, writing that 'I find it most distressing to believe in Liberal principles, but, at the same time, to be convinced that the present Government [the Conservatives had returned to power] may get us out of our difficulties, and that the Liberals may add to their troubles.'

Until 1952, when she was succeeded in the Chairmanship by

her niece, Mrs John Hare, the affairs of the Cowdray Club continued to give Trudie much work and worry. The Club's thirty year lease of its premises from the College of Nursing, which Lady Cowdray had arranged, expired in 1950. As the date approached Trudie needed all her tact and firmness to secure what she felt to be fair terms for the Club in the new lease.

'My dealings with the College,' she later wrote, 'have been rather difficult. . . . The College naturally wants money and the renewal of the lease presented considerable problems. My job, as Chairman of the Club, was to get the best terms possible so as to enable the Club to carry on. Eventually the College was convinced that my mother's gifts were made to the Club as well as to the College and that the points made as to the commercial value of the Club premises should, in fairness, be ignored. The rent to the Club was raised and a few rooms were taken over by the College, but on the whole the compromise is, I think, not bad.'

It was not until all the prolonged and difficult negotiations had been successfully completed that she felt free to resign the Club's Chairmanship.

Trudie remained a member of the Executive Committee of the Women's Institutes' National Federation and of several of its sub-committees until 1949. But even after she had resigned, 'because,' as she wrote, 'it is impossible to be a useful member of a Committee unless one is able to give enough time to master one or two branches of the work,' she was constantly being asked for advice and help, and her correspondence on Institute affairs continued until the end of her life. She remained, as she put it, 'a kind of honorary officer,' since Lady Albemarle had written to her 'we all agree that a Founder Chairman can have all sorts of special treatment without setting any precedents for the future.'

Always loyal to those who had served her, it was characteristic of Trudie that her first intervention, after her resignation from the Executive, should have been to try to secure for the administrative staff at headquarters a comparable increase in salaries to that given to the staff of the Women's Institute journal *Home and Country*. 'I thought I had written in the meekest terms,' one of her letters went, 'but I am delighted that you think I still have some guts left, and still more pleased that, when I mention a few of my views, you do not think I am being offensive.'

Two years later she showed that her fighting spirit was as strong as ever. An 'urgency resolution' was to be put forward by the Executive to the 1952 Annual General Meeting proposing that, because of the state of the nation's finances, the Executive should be empowered only to convene Annual General Meetings every other year. Trudie wrote to the Treasurer of the National Federation that she considered the proposal 'most dangerous, since the idle Institute will jump at it and arrange yet another outing with the money they save.' In a letter to her old friend Mrs Auerbach, the Institutes' former Treasurer, she said, 'I have been very careful not to interfere in W.I. matters for the last three or four years, as I have not felt energetic enough to do any work. However when I heard through my Institute of the "urgency resolution", it was too much for me.' After warning the Chairman that she intended to come to the Annual Meeting as a delegate from her local Stonehall Institute to speak against the resolution, and after canvassing some of the Counties for support, Trudie arrived at the Albert Hall. But the Executive's resolution was withdrawn. She had won her point. She spoke however on another resolution and presented the Denman Cup to the winners of that year. She had given this cup before the war to stimulate agriculture, and, since the war, had agreed that it should be awarded to the County Federation staging the best co-operative entry of preserved fruit and vegetables at the Dairy Show. This was the last Annual General Meeting that Trudie was to attend.

Her long experience of the value of proper procedure in a democratic organization and of the art of chairmanship—it was often said that she was the greatest living Chairman, man or woman—was a subject on which Trudie felt she could still be of use to the Institutes. In 1951 she was writing to the General Secretary, 'I have never before suggested my name as a speaker, but I just wonder if I could have half an hour at the Chairmen's Conference.' Needless to say her offer was 'hailed with joy'. At home at Balcombe she began to make notes for a pamphlet which

Presenting awards to Land Girls, World War II

Opening of Denman College, 1948
Left to right: Lady Brunner, Sir Richard Livingstone, Trudie

would sum up the practical knowledge she had gained. It was never written, but her notes show her approach to the subject. There are some on procedure—'its object, to give the minority a hearing but to ensure that the majority wins the day'; and there are amusing specimen resolutions from 'a normal W.I.', 'a slack W.I.', 'a growing W.I.', 'a stagnant W.I.', 'a gay W.I.', 'a small W.I.'—with suggestions on how to deal with them. Among the notes on Chairmanship are:

'A Chairman should exercise both impartiality and leadership; a Chairman is not a hostess, the two functions are quite separate . . . The duty of a Chairman is to obtain the views of the shy and silent and make the *rest* keep to the point . . . Never assume that any member of the Committee is a half-wit. . . . It is no good for a Chairman to try to hurry people. She must be content to sow new ideas and they will flower next time. . . . You must look ahead for promising people; I assure you there is nothing more satisfactory than discovering talent and giving responsibility to new people.'

Denman College was another great interest. It had not been easy to find suitable premises for the new Women's Institute College, and Trudie had been active in helping over the survey of possible houses and had allowed her credit to be pledged in making offers. Eventually, in 1947, Marcham Park near Abingdon in Berkshire was purchased. Once the home of the notorious eighteenth-century miser, John Elwes, it had been entirely rebuilt by his granddaughter about 1820, and is a pleasant Georgian mansion with handsome rooms and finely timbered grounds. The Carnegie United Kingdom Trust had given £20,000 towards the purchase and conversion of the house, while the Institutes set themselves a target of £60,000 for their donations. In fact, these now total £70,000, of which £40,000 has been put to an endowment fund. Post-war rationing and restrictions made the alterations, furnishing and equipment a formidable task. But gifts came in from many sources at home and abroad. Some County Federations undertook the furnishing of bedrooms, each distinctively carried out with fine craftsmanship. Others presented equipment such as china and blankets. With Lady Brunner (who was to succeed Lady Albemarle as the National Federation's Chairman in 1951) as the moving spirit of the enterprise, difficulties were somehow overcome and, in September 1948, the College was officially opened by Sir Richard Livingstone. It was he who, at a Conference in 1943, had first suggested that the Institutes might solve many of their educational needs and difficulties by establishing their own college. Trudie, of course, was at the opening and also spoke.

The College was exceptionally fortunate in its first warden, Miss Elizabeth Christmas. The atmosphere which she created contains no breath of an 'Institution'. Instead, there is a friendly elegance and distinction which would have been especially commended by Trudie, whose portrait, painted by Anthony Devas after the war when she was very ill, is the first thing that the visitor sees as he enters the hall.

In the ten years since Denman College was opened, 21,000 Institute members have attended courses there. There is now accommodation for sixty resident students, and the 160 courses which take place each year from Mondays to Fridays or over the week-end reflect all the activities which the Institute movement has fostered since its early days. Music, drama, agriculture and horticulture, food preservation and cooking, handicrafts, public questions and international affairs all have their part, as well as such subjects as civics, health, painting and modelling, local and social history, poetry and the novel. There are 'A' courses for helping the ordinary Institute member to learn the elements of new skills and to acquire a wider educational background; and there are more advanced 'B' courses for those who will subsequently instruct others. These four-day courses cannot, of course, enable subjects to be studied in any great depth, nor is perfection in craft skills likely to be acquired in so short a time. But Denman College has also a wider purpose, and a country housewife's whole outlook is enlarged by the experience—often a completely novel one—of staying away from home at the College and, free from domestic cares, of pursuing her own special interests in company with like-minded countrywomen from all over England and Wales.

Such is the countrywomen's College which bears Trudie's name. It would be hard to conceive a memorial more in keeping with one of the great objects of her life and work.

(iii)

The one public activity to which Trudie continued wholly to devote herself until the end of her life was the Family Planning Association. Unlike the sturdy and long established Institutes, it was a delicate plant, still not firmly rooted and needing, she felt, all the help and courage that she could give it. In spite of her ill-health, therefore, she continued as Chairman of the Association's Executive Committee, with Margaret Pyke, as Honorary Secretary, taking as much work as possible off her shoulders. Trudie regularly presided at the Executive Committee's monthly meetings in London and at the Association's Annual General Meetings. She also took the Chair at such events as the International Congress which the Association organized in 1948 at Cheltenham on 'Population and World Resources in relation to the family'. It was, too, her financial assistance that enabled the Association that year to buy new and much larger headquarters premises at 64 Sloane Street so as to allow for the Association's steady expansion.

A landmark in the Association's history was set up in 1949 when the Royal Commission on Population published its Report. It stated, *inter alia*, that contraceptive knowledge was one of the conditions of the great social advances of the age, helping to free women from excessive burdens and to ensure that more and more of the children born were wanted children and not the result of ignorance; that public policy should seek to encourage the spread of voluntary parenthood; and that the giving of advice on contraception to married persons who wanted it should be accepted as a duty of the National Health Service, and the existing restrictions on the giving of such advice by public authority clinics should be removed.

There could hardly have been a more complete vindication of all the views that Trudie had so courageously pioneered over so many years. Although the Report was never discussed by Parliament it was, of course, of the greatest value to the Family Planning Association who at once proceeded to make full use of such authoritative recommendations in support of its programme. Trudie herself presided at the Press Conference which the Association held on the day of the Report's publication.

Since then, the growth of the national and international influence of the Family Planning Association has been spectacular. In 1949 there were ninety-one branch clinics dealing with 40,000 new patients a year. Today the clinics number over 300, attended yearly by 350,000 patients. Neither Trudie, nor Lord Horder, the wise physician who was the Association's President and to whom, on the medical side, it owed so much, lived to celebrate the Association's Silver Jubilee in 1955, when the seal of official recognition was set on the Association's work by a visit to its headquarters from the Minister of Health and by his declaring that 'I believe that you do an admirable work and indeed my presence here today shows that.' In the Church the climate of opinion had so altered that the Report of the 1958 Lambeth Conference was to state that it was wrong to say that, in marriage, sexual intercourse ought not to be engaged in except with the willing intention to procreate children; and that 'Christians have every right to use the gifts of science for proper ends.' And with what an amused reflection on how times had changed would Trudie have greeted the leading article in *The Times* in 1959, which, in condemning the Council of the British Medical Association for rejecting an advertisement of the Family Planning Association for one of its journals, apparently in deference to pressure from Roman Catholic doctors, stated that 'by general recognition of the majority in this country, the Family Planning Association has taken its place among the respectable and useful adjuncts of the Social Services.'

In the words that the Minister of Health used in 1955, the position that the Family Planning Association holds today would have been 'unthinkable to the pioneers of the movement, and unthinkable only a few years ago.' In saying this, the Minister rightly referred to Lady Denman as the Association's 'founder and inspirer'. Without her financial help the Association could never have existed. Without her wisdom and judgement, her wide experience and prestige it could not, in so short a time, have achieved such recogntion and such success.

(iv)

Trudie's London home at 43 Upper Grosvenor Street had been requisitioned during the war. Immediately afterwards she sold the lease, but kept the Mews garage and flat. This provided a very useful family *pied-à-terre*, but when she visited London Trudie herself usually stayed with her brother Clive and his wife.

At Balcombe the household had changed soon after the war with the retirement on pension of the old head servants. But with the aid of some replacements and of 'dailies', Trudie was still able to retain in fair measure the character and comfort of her home. Margaret Pyke, living at Balcombe, gave her constant companionship, while old friends such as Lady Wavell, Lady Sanderson, Joy Winn and Mark Grant-Sturgis were again frequent week-end visitors, and Nellie Grant would stay when she came on holiday from Kenya. Lord Denman was now happily settled in a Victorian villa in Hove, looked after by a devoted companion. They would often come over to Balcombe for the day, and when Denman had to have an operation, Trudie at once went to Hove to take charge.

Arthritis gradually compelled Trudie to abandon golf, but she still played skilful and vigorous table-tennis. There was, too, the novelty of television to watch, and when she was forced to lead a less active life, she turned more to books. It was, however, in her daughter and her grandchildren that Trudie found her greatest interest in her last years. Nothing had pleased her more during the war than the way in which Judith not only took on, with conspicuous success, the County Chairmanship of the West Sussex Women's Land Army and membership of the County War Agricultural Executive, but also, in her husband's absence at the war, ran his large estate. After the war, it was a very pleasant relief for Trudie to have her daughter take financial matters into her competent hands and so to straighten out the complicated tax position as to make it possible for Balcombe to be maintained.

Then there was the fun of watching the four grandchildren grow up—Penelope the eldest, born in 1932, on whom she had doted since her birth; the twins Raymond and Rona born in 1934; and Mark, the youngest, born in 1937, who lived at Balcombe in the latter part of the war. With her Land Army and her estate responsibilities, Judith had little time to devote to her children. Penelope was at boarding school, but Mark, left largely in a nurse's hands at an impressionable age, had become very difficult to manage. Trudie much enjoyed taking in hand the small boy whose red hair matched hers. 'He has many of the qualities of a great man,' she told her daughter, 'but they are not pleasant in the home!' The result, however, of Mark's being placed in Trudie's charge was very satisfactory, and when any of the grandchildren developed tiresome habits, Trudie would recommend the best form of treatment, reassuring their mother that such things were only passing phases. The grandchildren were always delighted when they knew that they were going to Balcombe to see their granny; and, as they grew older, their letters to her from school or holidays, many of which she kept, show how freely and naturally they confided in her, and how close yet undemanding was her interest in them.

In 1953 Trudie had the excitement of the weddings of both her granddaughters. She greatly enjoyed having young parties of her granddaughters' friends to stay at Balcombe for these occasions and even played billiard fives with them. She was particularly pleased that both granddaughters were to make their married homes near Balcombe, Penelope at Stonehall which Trudie handed over to her with the home farm. Although Balcombe Place itself is now a boys' preparatory school, her granddaughter carries on from Stonehall Trudie's traditions of the management of the Balcombe estate.

During 1953 Trudie's health had seemed to be better, but early in 1954 she had two sharp attacks of illness with much pain and high fever. The doctors found that the trouble came from

Portrait by Anthony Devas, 1951

the displacement of an organ. It was yet another legacy from 1936. Trudie was greatly pleased that the doctors had discovered the cause of her attacks, even if the remedy necessitated another major operation. She knew that this would involve a considerable risk to her life, but she never for a moment hesitated in deciding to have the operation performed, saying, 'I've no wish to remain alive feeling C3; and if the operation is successful, I shall feel fit again.'

The operation took place on June 1st. Trudie stood it well. Next morning the good news was telephoned to the Executive Committee of the Women's Institutes' National Federation who were in session immediately before the start of the Annual General Meeting. All the members signed a note to her to tell her of their relief and to wish her a good recovery. But a little later her heart suddenly collapsed, and she died peacefully unconscious. As she would have wished, the news was kept from the Annual General Meeting, and the delegates only knew of it when they read the evening papers as they dispersed at the end of the day. That evening the first Executive of the new Institute year met as usual, but little business was done. A member wrote of their 'extraordinary feeling of sorrow', and how 'only love could have inspired that deep emotion that swept all of us.'

The hundreds of letters of sympathy that were written, as well as expressing admiration for Trudie's achievements, all voiced the sense of personal loss, even the letters from individual Institutes whose members only knew her as the guiding spirit of their movement. 'Our very dear friend;' or 'we do not know of anyone who will be mourned by so many or so greatly missed;' or 'so long as there are Women's Institutes, so long will the Denman tradition endure;' or 'our gratitude for having enriched the lives of so many thousands of countrywomen and brought them untold happiness', were typical expressions. The writers spoke, too, of their sense of Trudie's greatness and of the rare quality of her character. 'She was one of the few really big people' was one expression; another was, 'they say all power corrupts; she had power and was never corrupted by it, and think she is the only person I have ever known who had the strength of character to resist it.' 'Her courage and integrity in public life, and the selfless service which she gave with such wisdom and humanity especially to the cause of all women,' was how Queen Elizabeth the Queen Mother desired her 'high regard and admiration' to be expressed.

In accordance with Trudie's wish, her body was cremated and the ashes scattered at Balcombe. A week later a memorial service was held in Balcombe Parish Church, which was filled with a great company of people. Dr Bell, the Bishop of Chichester, paid a moving tribute of remembrance. Although, as he said,

> 'she refused to call herself a member of the Church and took no part in its worship,' yet it seemed to him 'not unfitting as we look back on her life and record of devoted self-giving, that her many friends who are members of the Church, as well as those who are not, should meet together to offer their tribute and join in memorial prayer in Balcombe Parish Church.'

Speaking with insight into her character Dr Bell said,

> 'if "shy" is the right term for the opposite of pushing oneself upon another personality, there was a certain quality of shyness about Lady Denman. Yet no one could be more completely at home than she was with those who understood the meaning of personal contact or were in need of wise counsel, and she was miserable if she offended anybody. . . . None who knew her intimately were in doubt of her deep affection. To her own children and grandchildren she was a marvellous mother and grandmother, a tower of strength and unfailing in her understanding and love. In her public life there was one great motive by which her work was directed—the determination to do everything she could to help the women of her country. She sought, so far as it lay in her power, to prevent them being trampled upon. She was also resolved to secure that, with the help of a sound education and in other ways, they should have every opportunity for the development of their gifts, and for making their full contribution to the life of the community as citizens and countrywomen, as wives and mothers. Lady Denman had a profound belief in the principles of democracy. She trained herself, and (it may be truthfully said) to a considerable extent educated herself, in the practice of these

principles when she was quite a young woman, and held them to the end. . . . To the end of her life she was valiant for the truth which she saw, and set an example in her human love, her service to others and her concern for justice, from which all who knew and loved her may profit. She has left a name behind her which will not be forgotten.'

Both the Women's Institutes and the Family Planning Association established memorials to her. The Institutes initiated a 'Lady Denman Memorial Fund' to which almost every Institute gladly subscribed. The £14,000 thus raised in small subscriptions was applied as to £6,000 for building the Lady Denman dining-hall at Denman College, the remaining money being divided between the College building fund and the endowment of 'Denman' bursaries for Institute members attending courses on agriculture or organization at the College.

The Family Planning Association's memorial took the form of 'Lady Denman Memorial Clinics', set up in small market towns serving wide rural areas. Such clinics needed assistance from a special fund, since they could not be expected to be as self-supporting as clinics in the cities. The first of the memorial clinics was opened at Northallerton in September 1955 and was quickly followed by others. Although the target for the fund was £5,000, over £9,000 has been raised, and there are now twenty-five Lady Denman memorial clinics. Their association with a name so trusted by countrywomen has greatly helped to give confidence in their services, and they are fulfilling Trudie's special wish that family planning advice and help should be available to country-women as well as to townswomen.

Almost at the hour at which Trudie died, the Albert Hall was echoing to the sound of 6,000 countrywomen singing Blake's 'Jerusalem' to Parry's noble music. The song ended:

> 'I will not cease from mental fight,
> Nor shall my sword sleep in my hand,
> Till we have built Jerusalem
> In England's green and pleasant land.'

It was a verse which Trudie had so often joined in singing with her fellow Institute members, in little village halls, at County gatherings and, year after year, so movingly in the great assembly in the Albert Hall. Although she herself might have smiled at Blake's words, they nevertheless truly expressed the resolve with which, from the beginning, she had sought to imbue the Institute Movement; and it was in their spirit that she had lived her own life. For fifty years her mind and her sword had been given, without reserve and without thought of self, to building her concept of the material and spiritual Jerusalem which she so passionately believed to be the just and rightful heritage not only of country-women, but of all women; and no one woman's work or example had ever done more to achieve the words' high purpose.

INDEX

Index

[A]